Psychological Warfare

The Most Effective Techniques For Fighting And Winning

(How To Always Keep The Upper Hand On Anyone Psychologically)

Joan Garcia

Published By **John Kembrey**

Joan Garcia

Psychological Warfare: The Most Effective Techniques For Fighting And Winning (How To Always Keep The Upper Hand On Anyone Psychologically)

ISBN 978-1-77485-591-1

No part of this guidebook shall be reproduced in any form without permission in writing from the publisher except in the case of brief quotations embodied in critical articles or reviews.

Legal & Disclaimer

The information contained in this ebook is not designed to replace or take the place of any form of medicine or professional medical advice. The information in this ebook has been provided for educational & entertainment purposes only.

The information contained in this book has been compiled from sources deemed reliable, and it is accurate to the best of the Author's knowledge; however, the Author cannot guarantee its accuracy and validity and cannot be held liable for any errors or omissions. Changes are periodically made to this book. You must consult your doctor or get professional medical advice before using any of the suggested remedies, techniques, or information in this book.

Upon using the information contained in this book, you agree to hold harmless the Author from and against any damages, costs, and expenses, including any legal fees potentially resulting from the application of any of the information provided by this guide. This disclaimer applies to any damages or injury caused by the use and application, whether directly or indirectly, of any advice or information presented, whether for breach of contract, tort, negligence, personal injury, criminal intent, or under any other cause of action.

You agree to accept all risks of using the information presented inside this book. You need to consult a professional medical practitioner in order to ensure you are both able and healthy enough to participate in this program.

Table of contents

Introduction

It's easy to batter anyone with a knife baseball bat or any other physical objects. The person you batter can be injured physically without difficulty. However, you are usually facing murder or assault charges. Additionally, someone might harm you in self-defense. Injuring someone physically can lead to several risks that are typically not worth the tiny bit of satisfaction you can get.

Therefore, if you're looking to hurt someone you love, it's usually better to go with more subtle strategies. "What subdued method can I employ?" you may ask in your look for a way to end your relationship with your ex. You might not wish to hurt any person, yet you would like to be a success around the globe. There are always people fighting with you or ignoring you, and you're hoping to be successful. What can you do to win this?

The answer is to use psychological warfare. Through psychological warfare, you are able to employ manipulation, words, and even propaganda to thwart your adversaries and bring the control of your enemies. You can force people to do what you wish by employing various psychological tricks and strategies. It is not necessary to have any kind of strength or even any allies to work this to your advantage. The best part about psychological warfare is that it is possible to complete it by yourself, with your own abilities and abilities.

Psychological warfare is not a joke. You can easily beat people mentally until they are completely broken. You can achieve great control over your opponents using the techniques of psychological combat. The greatest part? You won't be facing any jail time or the threat of physical injury. There aren't any laws against psychological warfare, and nobody is likely to believe you are doing anything wrong. This is, if you use psychological warfare correctly.

There is no need to be concerned about doing the right thing. This book will show you all you must be aware of. Through these pages you'll be taught the finer details of subtlely and effectively getting control over the mind of a person. By employing the most subdued strategies for mental control, you are able to create havoc in the mind of someone. It's like inciting war against someone's mind as well as increasing your odds of winning.

By engaging in psychological warfare, you're applying the principles that govern human behavior to your benefit. This means that you're almost certain to succeed. Many people react to certain tips and tricks in the same way using them, and implementing these techniques will yield the success you desire. You will surely beat the odds with your mind instead of using brute force.

The use of psychological warfare calls you to be precise and calculating. You could launch attacks on individuals who are not ready for. They aren't able to anticipate psychological attacks. There is the possibility in the form of surprise that you can use to your advantage.

Psychological warfare is more sly than you could ever imagine. The person you are targeting and his family members and friends may be aware that something is not right however they won't be able to prove that you are to be guilty of any crime. It is likely that your the mental control of your mind is much more secure than control of the physical, so you are able to really destroy your victim.

With aplomb and delicacy you are able to win the fight against someone, and come out as the winner. You can conquer people without putting an effort to combat. You can then control the situation and are invincible.

When war is raging between nations and governments, their physical aspect is quite obvious. We see the bombings, deaths and body counts. What they don't see is the psychological aspect of conflict. It is possible to win over enemies or subdued by using extremely subtil and clever tricks like flyers that spread propaganda messages that make people against their government. Even soldiers handing out candy to children in villages of enemy nations are using a method that is known as psychological warfare. Psychological warfare is the type of warfare that usually wins wars in the quiet. The greatest part is that nobody is aware. It's so subtle and secretive because it's completely mental.

It is believed that the United States is especially adroit in the field of psychological conflict. There's a reason this United States is one of the most powerful nations on the planet. Even without going to war every day

The United States is able to maintain control over a variety of countries through trade and propaganda. If you take lessons directly from those who work for the United States government, you will be able to prepare yourself to be successful in using secret psychological strategies to win all your personal fights. The people will not be aware of how you're working as you control their minds, and even their hearts. At the end of the day you will prevail without ever going to battle. Your victims will not know what transpired to them. They'll essentially surrender control and be submissive to you on their own free will.

Doesn't it sound incredible to have that type of power? It's amazing. However, the information in this book should not be dismissed lightly. This is your single and only caution. If you follow these strategies you will get rapid and reliable outcomes. You can be in control of one person, and you could make someone break. This book is for your enemies, not your family members.

A lot of the techniques described inside this volume were developed in the US government as well as other agencies including the KGB. They are tested and tried. This makes them more risky. Your adversaries should be afraid right now, since you are learning the most effective weapon available.

Chapter 1: What Exactly Is Psychological Warfare?

What is it?

It is the than just a war that is fought in the mind. It's very sneaky due to its power as well as its inscrutable nature. A lot of people don't realize that they are victims of psychological warfare until they are aware of the indicators and methods. Psychological warfare is the use of subtil methods to influence or alter a person's attitudes, beliefs and behavior, ultimately controlling the person from a distance. If you're in control of someone's mental and physical actions you are able to exert enormous power over that person. You can force someone to perform whatever you want to.

Psychological warfare employs a wide range of tactics to deter the enemy. It is possible to use audio and light to trigger subliminal effects in your opponent's mind. You can make use of propaganda or rumors as well as other types of public information to influence the decisions of someone else. It is possible to damage a person's reputation and also their trust. Through a myriad of mental, physical and emotional techniques that you can take control over someone, and even ruin the life of someone. The best techniques of psychological warfare will be discussed in greater detail in subsequent chapters.

Psychological warfare is generally superior to any other kind of attack. It is not just possible to hide completely and undetected, but you also cause real damage. There are no laws that prohibit psychological combat.

There are many other terms for psychological warfare. They are PSYOP (Psychological Operation) (Psychological Operations), heart and mind propaganda, political war as well as MISO (Military Information Support Operation). These names will give you an indication the fact that it is an incredibly popular tactic used in the army. The government uses psychological warfare in battle and in intelligence as it is extremely effective and extremely discreet.

Real Life Applications

There are four main reasons to use psychological warfare. The first is that it can be used to force foreigners and government officials to adopt positions that are favorable

8

to the government of the invader. For example for instance, the United States could convince the people of an African nation to dislike its own administration. Then, the people begin an uprising, which eventually disintegrates the government. They can then invade the United States. United States can then easily invading the country, under the pretense of offering "aid" and profiting due to the fact the army is focused on the uprising to stop the threat of invasion.

Psychological warfare is the second. It involves strategically-planned attacks of terror to subdue a group. Random violence or espionage as well as other techniques create a state of fear and anxiety. They are more likely to take on whatever is necessary to obtain some kind of relief. A dictator or government can profit from situations that people are afraid simply by promising protection.

Thirdly, hypnosis, brainwashing as well as other forms of manipulation and control of the mind are used to alter other peoples their personalities and perspectives. People become instruments and are altered or altered according to their own preferences.

9

The media and the government are able to work together to alter the views of the majority of the people.

In addition, psychological warfare could be employed to influence the mindset of entire groups. One example is the way in which American people were taught to be averse to terrorists, without completely understanding the target was. What is a terrorist? They are Muslim extremists or are they also different groups of people? The government uses this model to influence public opinion and win the necessary support for war. Governments have the power to influence their citizens to support an issue, even if the government actually has an motive. In the case of the terrorist It is believed that the American hate of terrorists was employed as a tool by government officials of the US government to win the support of the public for an oil conflict that was fought in the Middle East. Although this is certainly an issue of opinion but it's an illustration of how a government is able to gain support from its citizens to pursue a political agenda however, it really has a completely differentand secret motive to want war.

Each of these strategies is utilized by

governments in the real world. But, you are able to adapt the methods to suit your personal needs. There are many ways to adapt tactics of the military psychological warfare every day to suit their own agendas.

You can employ methods of instigation and troublemaking to cause people to hate one others or their idols. It is possible to change their beliefs. If you disable the social supports and beliefs systems of individuals and removing the things that make them strong. The people will be in confusion without the structures they have built to protect their minds.

It is possible to use terror to intimidate individuals. When your adversaries are scared they are scared, you hold the supreme power. You can give them a sense of relief if they take action for you, or intimidate them by using threats. Fear can be an effective motivational tool.

You can also alter the personality of individuals to meet your needs. You can train people into becoming automatons under your control. As time passes, you can influence them to give up convictions and values that are against your own personal goals. At the end of the day you'll have the ultimate mental and emotional slave.

You can also use a covert method to get people to support causes, and in the process, serve up secret agendas you've got. For example, you can convince people to contribute to your cause by convincing that you're supporting the cause they're enthusiastic about. People don't realize that your organization was created to provide tax benefits to politicians.

The news and media industry is frequently guilty of using psychological warfare. Coverage of the presidential election is a good example of how media organizations attempt to employ tactics of psychological warfare including propaganda in order to get voters to support the candidate they believe is most suitable. Tom Brokaw is one news anchor who has been accused of subliminally inducing voters to support certain Republican candidates each year. While not intending to influence voters, Brokaw would dedicate a certain amount of energy to the candidates he liked, but without making these candidates appear into a more attractive light. His viewers were already mostly Republican in their voting habits, had more likely to vote for the candidates he favored following his television shows.

Many people aren't aware about the intricacies of psychological combat. This is part of what makes it so effective. It's mostly hidden which means that enemies are in the dark and unaware. They are unaware the government or another person is targeting them. People simply think that they are pressured to do the right thing. They get excited and devoted to cause without knowing the deeper motives behind the motives. The deliberate deception of individuals is a devious and virtually foolproof method to influence people's psychological state to further your private goals.

The government employs psychological warfare to control its citizens and other nations citizens. However, you can also use psychological warfare to take control of those in your life. The usage in your home for psychological warfare is comparable with the use of military forces however, your goal is likely to either get your way or hurt the person you love. You could adapt the techniques employed by the federal government to ensure that psychological warfare works for you in a private situation.

There are numerous personal advantages from psychological combat. Utilizing the second-guessing and manipulation, deceit persuasion, torture, and deceit tips within this guide, you will be able to achieve whatever you wish. You can psychologically harm people until they cease to be threat to you. You can influence and convince people to do whatever you'd like. You can make them wish to meet you or become friends due to your influence over them. Your enemies will turn into your friends or your friends and everyone will fear you and will respect your decisions.

Find out the methods to modify techniques of the government in order to make use of psychological warfare for your advantage.

The History of Psychological Warfare

It is difficult to pinpoint the exact timeframe of psychological warfare because it has been utilized by individuals and by governments throughout time. The psychological element of warfare is something is often overlooked by people however, it has always been present. It is believed to have been an element in every conflict from the very first time conflict began. Humans are susceptible to violence and conflict which means that the practice of this type of warfare is quite old in fact. Humans have long recognized the effectiveness of psychological warfare, and have discovered that it is an effective partner to physical combat.

British historian and military analyst J.F.C. Fuller first invented the term "psychological warfare" in the year 1920. The actual idea behind psychological warfare, as well as the concept itself, didn't become popular in the late 1950s. The tactics used by the war in WWII led to the public's fascination in the field. What exactly was psychological warfare was unclear in the beginning. Today, it's not a completely known or understood issue. Certain people attribute the techniques of psychological warfare solely to the military and conflict, while some believe it is due to psychological abuse and tactics can be used on a personal basis. This latter interpretation is the one we have chosen to employ in this book.

The psychological warfare method is long-standing that it's difficult to identify who developed it. The entire human race could be believed to have originated this technique, given that governments from every culture have used it throughout the history of mankind. In Sun Tzu's The Art of War is an ancient work that describes the various tactics of psychological warfare that were employed by the Chinese military used in The 500 BCs and beyond.

Psychological warfare is more frequent in our worldwide access to the media. Everyone around the world has access to more information about what's happening around the world. It's no longer difficult to research perspectives on crucial global issues. The mainstream media has lost control over how people get information, due to the rise of media sites like WikiLeaks. The psychological aspects of war, propaganda and secret government plans are becoming more prominently known to the public.

Although World War II certainly popularized this notion among the masses however, it is the Cold War is the best instance of psychological warfare in action accessible. Learning about The Cold War is practically like studying a guide on how to carry out psychological warfare. In the Cold War, both United States and Soviet Union both took psychological warfare and economic warfare into the highest level during their fierce race to dominate during the 50s and 60s.

The principal psychological tactic both sides employed during the Cold War was fear. The people lived in fear of a nuclear attack imminently approaching. Underground bomb shelters and bomb shelters were built across both the United States and the Soviet Union to prepare. The chilling cartoons produced during this period reflected the intense emotions of the time.

It is believed that the Soviet Union and United States both had a reputation as broadcasters of white noise. People who listened to the broadcasts mistakenly thought that it was as encryption, and devoted a lot of time and money in encryption of broadcasts, but for nothing. They also hired spies who appeared so innocent, that doubt was created for innocent people and suspicion for spies grew. Psychotherapy, torture and other methods were often and brutally used on captured spies to try to collect as numerous identities of its spies that they could. Secret agents abound, causing the fear and anger of secretiveness. The war was mostly played out with emotion, and no side knew what the other side was truly doing.

In Gulf War and the War against Terrorism Psychological warfare played a significant part. Brochures designed to incite fear into the hearts of the civilian population were circulated to urge individuals to flee their homelands or to rebel against their government. The spread of stories and rumors was intended to create terror, fear, and fear. Bombings, both strategic and violent, were frequently used for breaking the adversary's desire down. Additionally, US troops were known to broadcast in a rousing manner that urged enemies who were hiding to get out and fight. The feelings of fear, anger and despair were employed extensively to harm Middle Eastern enemies.

The global access to information on the Internet television, radio has made the art of psychological warfare more accessible than ever before. There are a variety of tools in the media to start a war on your mind regardless of whether it's in a personal or a political scale. A lot of people are able to access the media, and they take in its news without questioning. They believe in the propaganda and lie without looking for more proof. Thus, it is easy to employ subliminal signals and outright lies to convince people to believe in your beliefs.

The media is skilled at providing a fake truth to viewers. The majority of people believe the information they get from the news is accurate. They don't realize of the fact that they are being manipulated by powerful forces that they aren't conscious of. For example, Baghdad Bob was an Iraqi diplomat who provided daily news briefings about the situation in the war. He deceived the Iraqi populace, telling them that they were winning the battle and that Baghdad was protected from nuclear attacks. The majority of people from his country as well as the nearby Middle Eastern nations saw him talking on television and believed in him. The Baghdad bombings were an astonishment to the majority of people because of.

The power of wildfire in Internet hoaxes is another instance of how people be influenced by anything they see in the media given to them. Certain hoaxes, like the myth that people accidentally consume eight spiders each year while sleeping are widely spread on all over the Internet as well as being taken by Internet users as facts. A lot of people are able to access media, including on the Internet with no doubt.

The ability to influence and control people using the media and news outlets because people believe in the information they hear. The anchors in the news have created an amount of authority. They therefore exercise that authority, and the majority of people accept their statements as true. However, in reality, media is capable of, and is well-known for, manipulating the news in certain ways and deciding the content they present to give a meticulously planned perception of reality which may not be accurate. People are attracted and compelled to take certain behaviors and feelings by what they see. People can be influenced by their surroundings to support a particular political party, for example or fooled into believing an illusion of security over their country's successes in conflict.

Furthermore to that, the Internet can be a fantastic tool to defame an individual's reputation, which is an effective tactic to fight psychological warfare that we'll discuss in more depth later. The people who use the Internet are not strangers, so their social media profiles and business pages are the first impressions they make. If they don't make a good impression of themselves through your online profiles, it could be detrimental to their career as well as their private lives. There are many ways to share embarrassing photos or negative reviews and false information to undermine the online reputation of someone. This could negatively impact an individual's career and work prospects. Cyberbullying is also known as cyberbullying. the Internet provides a wide-ranging playing field where you can transform someone's reputation to something negative. It's also a place that you can publish items that could harm someone's feelings.

Hacking and cyberattacks are now also feasible. It is possible to obtain private and embarrassing information on the person you are talking to. The Internet lets you track people and obtain the details and personal information of their friends. You can also read their "private" messages and chat messages with astonishing ease. There is so much to learn about them that you could befriend them without much effort. Through dropping clues or taking control of the computer of someone else You can make them feel as if they're running around in circles.

The present Information Age is undoubtedly the most convenient and efficient opportunity to cause chaos on someone, or the entire world. Utilize the wealth of technological tools available to penetrate the media or the life of someone else.

The evidence of the fact that Psychological Warfare Works

The fact that psychological warfare is not a time-bound combat is a sign of its efficacy. The numerous governments that have utilized psychological warfare for centuries demonstrate that it is effective. Governments wouldn't rely as much on the psychological war if they were not as efficient. Sun Tzu's book The Art of War is often hailed as a definitive strategy for winning battles.

The current Iraqi war is an instance of how psychological warfare has been successful. Through a variety of methods that have been employed, government officials from the US government has successfully used propaganda to create the fear of hatred and resentment in both the US as well as Islamic countries. In the meantime, Islamic terrorists have effectively made a mess across various countries, including the US, Israel, France as well as other nations through specific terror attacks as well as suicide bombings. Today, all nations live in constant fear of attack. This is a part of the mental torture terrorist organizations seek to create.

You've likely experienced psychological warfare in your own life. Consider the person in your workplace or household who is capable of getting you to do what they want. The person you are thinking of is likely to be great in expressing opinions that scare you or cause you to doubt your own abilities. It is possible that you have friends who are trying to ruin your routine with their savage actions and you're afraid to voice your concerns because they're intimidating. You might have experienced bullying at school from one who could make you feel bad about your self and make you feel scared all every day. People who can modify your behavior and feelings through non-physical methods employ psychological torture on you. They've managed to exercise a great deal influence over your life and control of your life through manipulation your behavior.

It is evident from these individuals that psychological warfare actually works. However, now that you're convinced of its effectiveness you may be wondering what you could possibly do with it for yourself. The techniques that others utilize to control their emotions might seem a bit complicated. Most of the time, their strategies are too subtle to learn about. This is fine as this book will explain all you must be aware of.

In the year 1513 in 1513, an Italian diplomat and aristocrat named Niccolo Machiavelli wrote The Prince. The book is an exclusive guide on the ways to be calculated as well as manipulative and clever in order to rule the country and ultimately manage people. The Sun Tzu's Art of War is another guide. Both of these books are extremely old and demonstrate the respect that people for ages have had for psychological warfare. We will be referring to these texts whenever we teach you effective and beneficial methods and applications for psychological warfare.

Chapter 2: How To Determinate Your Occupant

In this section, tried and tested strategies for combating psychologically will be discussed in depth. These are the strategies which will definitely destroy your adversaries. These tips should not be taken lightly due to their extremely effective and real use in the psychological combat.

Primary Goals

If you're using psychological warfare There are four goals to be aware of. Focus on these four targets in order to have the benefits of success. Being distracted from these goals puts you at risk of being unable to control the power that mental warfare gives you.

The Mind

You must focus on controlling the mind of someone else. You should think of that mind as your goal instead of a person. Minds of people are the most important factor in his overall security. If you focus on the mind of the person, you will effectively control the individual.

It is easy to control your mind by controlling emotions. Thoughts can be difficult to control, however If you manage the emotions that trigger the thoughts of others, you can achieve total control over your thoughts. The key to achieving controlling your emotions is to manipulate the emotions of someone else through guilt, fear and obligation. Three of these emotions constitute the main emotions that let you have control over someone's actions and thoughts.

Fear is the most effective motivational force in the world. When you create fear on someone else, you are able to dramatically influence his actions. You can influence that person to take specific ways to be safe from threats. It is also possible to get him to be uncomfortable and decrease levels of happiness in his daily life. The most effective ways to trigger fear in others is by making one doubt his own self-worth or mental health, making them be afraid of his family members and causing someone to be afraid of being disliked. A decrease in self-esteem for someone else is a important way to create fear within him. The person will be worried about being unloved this is one of the most awful emotions a human is likely to be faced with. Humans can be described as herd animals, and they need love and attention.

Guilt can also cause people to take action. It is such a numb feeling that people perform amazing actions to avoid it. It is possible to make people feel guilty, even for sins that they didn't commit through pouting or showing the world how sorry you are. To alleviate the feelings of guilt, people take extreme measures to excuse themselves from their guilt. It is possible to profit from the guilt of someone else to convince them to perform your favor.

Obligation can be a great method to get people to follow your wishes. It can be a way to make people feel that they have a duty to do something to you, by giving them favors. As you show more favours to people, the greater amount of favors you show to make people feel more obliged, the more so you will make them feel. Someone who feels that you are in financial burden will be willing to go extraordinary efforts to settle the obligation. This is a form of reversing the idea of reciprocity, in which people swap a favor in exchange for a favor, or the equivalent of an eye.

The three emotions that make up what is known as the acronym FOG. FOG is a fitting acronym since it refers to a type of fog you can manipulate a victim's thoughts. Through FOG, you are able to cause someone to behave with certain behaviors. You don't have to be explicit that you're making use of FOG. FOG works because people be able to play into it. FOG is based on the natural human emotions.

Peace

When you try to disrupt peace of a person and peace, you can make him unhappy. People depend upon their tranquility and treasure it. Peace can be destroyed by many different ways. The mere act of making noise could disrupt people's peace. Inflicting uncomfortable feelings on people in social situations can disturb peace. People want to keep their tranquility and are willing to do everything to keep it from being disturbed.

Reputation

The majority of people are very cautious about their image. One's reputation determines what he's known by and how others view him. One may lose loved ones and friends as well as potential business opportunities in the event of a bad reputation. The reputation of someone else can create the impression that you are the sole source of their success. You could sever the person's family, friends and business connections through a negative impact on his reputation. The act of launching an attack on the reputation of someone else is punishable under law as slander or libel. However, you can get around this by being discrete in your slander or disseminating the truth. Many people have actual dirt on their records. In exposing this information it is legal to smear the reputation of someone and making him look less attractive before other peers.

Idols

Everyone needs an idol they can follow. The idols could be holy figures like saints and real people, such as famous or political leaders and even fake ones like fashion labels. People turn to their idols for guidance and protection. If you disable someone's idol, it could cause them to feel lost and confused, or even depressed with their life. It is easy to dismantle an idol by brainwashing him into turning to his demons. You can also ruin the image of idols to make people doubt in the idol. This was the case with OJ Simpson, as well as Michael Vick.

The Prince

Niccolo Machiavelli's book The Prince is an excellent essay on ways you can control others. The methods of Machiavelli are often manipulating, cunning and deceit. There is no physical act needed in the psychological battle. The Machiavellian ideas that he came up with led to the idea that is known as "Machiavellianism," which entails the use of covert tactics in order to gain personal gains. The opinions and feelings of other people do not matter when you are using Machiavellianism in order to get your desired outcome. Your focus is solely on your ultimate objective. The end justifies the means according to you. This is the essence of psychological conflict.

If you are using Machiavellian thinking you assume the role of a leader. You must think of you as the leader and take control of other people. Take control of your surroundings without hesitation and the rest of the individuals are in your hands. This is how you begin to unleash the psychological warfare of the other.

Don't worry about the opinion of your subordinates

There is no need to be a slave to anyone's moment of the day. The opinions of others aren't important. Don't make decisions in the light of the consensus of other people, or you'll look weak. Instead, you should make your own decisions and disregard the opinions of other people. You will appear more powerful and be able to take more control of your life by not letting others control you through their ideas and opinions.

Make use of your power

If you're able to Don't be afraid make use of it. Insisting on or stalling your power makes your appearance weak. It will drain the power you have fast. It is essential to be in charge and begin making use of your power as soon as you are able to. Be respectful and let people know that you won't be degraded. Make quick decisions and assert your authority as soon as you receive it.

Don't forget to wash your hands.

If you find yourself in an issue that you have little about, don't reveal your ignorance. Lack of knowledge can only make you appear insignificant and cause you to lose respect. Instead do your best to get dirty without asking questions or taking up too much time. You'll gain knowledge quickly as you move through. Also, "just wing it."

Befriend weaker people and stay clear of the more powerful Ones

The less fortunate people in the world are those who seek friendship. In reality, they don't look for it, they require it. In leveraging this desperate need, you can draw weaker people to you. They'll be submissive to you as you provide them with the power that they lack. You can make weaker people in your life look towards you as a leader , and eventually they will be your loyal followers.

Protect what is truly important to You.

Find out what is most important and stand up for it. Get rid of the less important things. It is your responsibility to choose your fights. The world is full of fights, and some of them are just waste of time. Instead of fighting irrelevant battles, save your energy for major fights that really matter. This way, you will be able to fight for what you value most and crush others by engaging in your most formidable, top-of-the-line battle.

Be Well-presented

The way you present yourself is crucial. If you present yourself as an authority person you can make people more likely to trust and admire your authority. Make yourself appear as if you are always right, you're confident, and confident. Maintain a good posture, dress appropriately and be proud of your appearance. Talk as you wish to talk , and don't talk to anyone else and no one should be allowed to talk to you. Handshake with firmness and keep constant eye contact. These things all communicate that you're not a person to be played with. You must project confidence and authority if you wish to be admired in the world.

Be prepared to take on risk

Make it clear to the world that you're the boss by demonstrating courage in taking action, without hesitation about the risk of taking it. The risk is always there. Do not let it deter your progress or cause you to reconsider your choices. If you do, you grant the risk authority over you and you will appear unworthy in the eyes of your colleagues. Consider risk as a challenge that you are able to solve rather than something that causes terror in you.

As a great leader, you should inspire others to view risk as a problem to address, but also. Be a leader who is confident in taking risks. This makes you a respected leader.

Don't rely on luck

Luck isn't real. It's a fantasy. If you place your faith in luck, you grant others and things the power to influence you. Don't trust things that are out of your control. Make sure you are in control and take the necessary changes or accept the chance you wish to take. Only you can ensure the best outcome rather than luck.

Copy the best

You have to show yourself as the best you can to others to win respect, trust and respect. People will be willing to give anything for you if they think you're the top. If you aren't sure how to excel in your field take a look at other people who are successful. Copy successful and well-known leaders in your area of expertise or crime novel villains that are easy to lure and manipulate those around them.

Don't be afraid to bend the law

You are able to bend or over the rules that govern the social interactions, society and even conversation. When you do this you demonstrate to the world that you're yourself. You are the one who decides. Nobody can be in control of you or even the authorities, whether real or imagined by the society. You make the rules for yourself and you play according to those rules. Others will admire this, and they'll strive to follow your rules book to gain your respect.

Make use of the Milton Model

The Milton Model is a form of neuro-linguistic programming also called NLP. NLP requires models to influence people to behave according to certain behaviors. Milton Model: Milton Model is an NLP model that lets you talk in a vague manner to allow people to translate what they are thinking to your statements. You are open to interpretation. So, it is impossible for people to accuse you of making bad choices. You also have the ability to influence people without telling them directly to do something.

You can convince people to be in agreement with everything you have to say through this Milton Model. People will apply their own interpretation on your words, and afterward they'll agree with you. They aren't aware of what they're actually doing.

Meta Modeling

Additionally, NLP helps in the creation of models of the way people behave. You can alter how people behave by analyzing their language. People frequently speak because they are used to it. They'll say things such as "everyone," "never," and "always." It is rare that these words correct. If you question it when you hear these words and you are able to make them begin to doubt the meaning behind them. You can exert a lot of control over others by making them doubt the meaning of what they say. It is possible to make them begin to examine themselves in order to be more pleasant to you.

For example If someone says "Everyone is in love with my name!" you can disable his euphoria by asking "Are you certain that everyone loves you?" or "What is love according to your definition?" With these questions you can cause someone to doubt whether everyone likes him. The person will start to look at his words in front of you because he is afraid that you'll expose how he's incorrect.

Don't allow exaggeration or any other kind of extravagant self-expression. You can control people's behavior by questioning and analyzing everything they say in order to force them to think about their own self-worth. You're both getting control while destroying confidence in yourself.

Make use of Mirroring

It is possible to make people feel closer to you by having them subtilly imitate your body's language as well as gestures. It is not advisable to be explicit about it, because it can cause irritation to those around you. If you do it in a subtle way, and imitate their movements following a two-second break, you'll let people know that you are a fan of them. The people will try to please you to earn your respect.

One of the most effective methods to use mirroring is to lean towards the person who is talking to you. Lean toward them at the the exact angle they are leaning towards you. This establishes a unspoken, unconscious connection with them.

Representational Systems

Certain people are visual. They'll say things such as, "See what I mean?" Other people are more audio-oriented and will ask "Do You hear me?" Yet others may be more tactile and ask, "Do you feel what I'm talking about?" Listen to these signals to determine which representational, or sensory system individuals prefer. Talk to them in the system they prefer. This will let them feel as if they have relationship with you and they'll try to delight you even more.

Sun Tzu's Thirty-Six Strategies of Sun Tzu

The following pages contain the thirty-six strategies of psychological warfare that we will go over in depth. This is the heart of the matter and this section will show you how to engage in psychological combat. Although these tactics are mostly employed in the army, I've provided some modifications for personal use. You can modify any of these techniques to suit your own personal war.

These methods were gathered and explained in detail in a specific Chinese military document written by Sun Tzu from the Chinese Warring States Era which occurred between the years 403 to 221 BC. The exact date of this text is not known, however the purpose of this text is obvious: to eliminate the enemy. In spite of its age this text from the past remains relevant in the present day because of its brutality and ruthlessness. These tactics were employed by Chinese military throughout the history of ancient times and remain in use today. A lot of these strategies appear to be intuitive since they are an essential and accepted element of the warfare of the whole human race. The methods described in this document have one goal, which is to bring the enemy to pieces. The effectiveness of these strategies is a given, considering their indefatigability.

Knowing that these techniques come from the Chinese text is essential to comprehend the Chinese language. A lot of times the use of the use of a Chinese metaphor is employed to convey the message.

Make the Sky your own for the purpose of Cross the Ocean

It's more effective to be clear rather than being be sneaky. If you do sneak around and hide behind the scenes, you'll appear to be in the wrong. It could make you look like a criminal. If you conduct yourself clearly it will appear to be honest and honest. You will not be accused of any wrongdoing.

Besieged Wei for the purpose of Seize Zhao

There is no need to directly attack your opponent to harm him. Sometimes, attacking the things the person loves is much better. You could hurt someone and make their life difficult for him by taking away the things he cherishes most. Everybody has a weakness such as a spouse, child or a friend who is a great one or pet, a beloved spot, home.

This wisdom is derived from a period in Chinese history, where Wei's State Wei was able to take on Qi, the nation of Zhao. Qi, the state Qi was insufficiently strong to confront Wei's army directly and instead Qi was able to take over its capital city.

Kill using a borrowed knife

41

You can't tackle every battle on your own. Sometimes, scheming or convincing someone else to stand in your place can be efficient. You don't need to be the one to carry out the dirty work, but others could be held accountable for your deeds. Bribery threats, extortion, and even threats are all ways to persuade others to take on your side to your advantage. Utilize people such as mailmen, judges, or even the banker, to take on your foe. These everyday people are fantastic ways to make life challenging for the enemy.

This is particularly useful when you want to make someone mad. You could use the assistance of others to create a false reality that is a bit off with your victim's notion of what's real. Utilizing common people like clerks at the grocery store could help to cement the false reality and lead your victim to start doubting his credibility.

Substitute Leisure to Labor

It's a good idea to take a break and enjoy leisure. It might seem like an inefficient way to spend your time however it's actually the best way to put your forces for battle. When your opponent is spending energy and effort trying to take you down and you save your energy. And when your opponent is tired, you can easily attack.

Be patient and prepare your plan of attack, but don't let your adversaries know what you're thinking. The more organized your plan is, the higher your chance of winning.

Make Sound in the East Then Attack From the West

Try to distract your adversaries by using a feint to enable you to perform an attack in a different way and surprise him. Begin to make a clear move that he could expect to see you do, and then reverse and perform a move you didn't anticipate in any way.

For example, he may think that you are trying to steal his girlfriend's identity to harm him. Try to impress his girlfriend by playing games with her. He'll start focusing on securing the girl from you, and protecting his relationship and his guard will go down in other areas. You can then secretly expose that he's been behaving badly with his girlfriend. It could ruin the relationship of his and his reputation while not actually stealing his girlfriend.

Create something from Nothing

Utilizing the idea of feints, you can scare your opponent by making a feint. Repeat the feint over and over. He may react to the two previous feints, but not to the third. The person will believe that you're playing the fool. Therefore when you attempt this move, it isn't really a trick. It's the actual attack.

In the above scenario The third time you try to snare his girlfriend ought to be the one in which you actually take her away. You will be caught by surprise and will be shocked by the fact that your third attempt was actually the attack.

Take a house and set it on fire

If someone is weak, they are unable to fight you. It is then that you can defeat him and completely take him down. You must wait until your victim is injured by an event in his life like an untimely death in the family or financial loss. If his self-esteem is at its lowest and his resources and connections are the smallest, you stand the greatest chance of damaging him. The person will not have the usual defenses in place.

It is recommended to select victims who are the most vulnerable. If you choose a person that is sturdy and able, you are likely to get an excellent fight. People who are vulnerable are prone to holes which are easy to find and then pierce them with a sword metaphorically.

Get into to Passage of Chencang

The first step is to attack your opponent in the face with your most powerful and most powerful force. Next, you can use an additional, more terrifying attack to trap him. Your opponent is not able to handle two distinct attacks. He'll split his thoughts and resources to fight two enemies at the same time in confusion and disorientation. He can't be successful if he's all in the air fighting the battle.

You can apply this technique in real-life situations by your own efforts or the aid of a friend or colleague. The first step is to launch an attack on the person's reputation. While he frantically tries to repair the damage and dispel any rumors you've created about him, he'll not be ready the day that a close friend of yours starts to release negative information concerning him to the media. Then he'll be insane, trying to manage an effective damage control. He'll probably get too confused and desperate that he'll make some kind of mistake that could confirm the gossip you've been spreading about him. People will start to distrust him, and he will be unable to repair the damage.

This also refers to a particular piece of Chinese military time. General Liu Bang pretended to be fixing the roads in order that his army could advance into Guanzhong to strike Xiang Lu. Xiang Lu was in an illusion of security and believed that the road would require Liu Bang forever to complete the road repair. But, Liu Bang really had an army of two that was advancing through the passageway of Chencang. The second army was able to take Xiang Lu's fortress shock, and then ushered into Han Dynasty. Han Dynasty.

Watch the fire rage across the River

It is sometimes better to remain the final person in the area. In combat there is a chance that you won't be the only one fighting. Relax and let the rest of the group battle it out. Then , you can join into the fray as everyone else is exhausted and battered due to the fight. You are able to take all the broken pieces.

There are two advantages when you wait. One is that you appear as you are a friend. Your target may believe you're an ally since you're not involved in the conflict. He'll allow you to be part of his inner circle and be able to trust you.

The other advantage is that everyone is weakened at the time you launch your move. There will be virtually no resistance when you go into. A few of the tasks will even be completed by the property.

This is especially useful when a large group of people engage in a war against one individual. It's also helpful when one person has provoked the hatred of a number of individuals. Then let others destroy the victim's thoughts. Then you'll be able to take the strike of grace.

Put a Knife in a smile

This is among the oldest tricks you can find in the book. Smile and conceal the knife you are using in your back. Give your enemy a warm welcome by appearing sweet and as if you are an all-around friend. You can make your adversaries feel secure in your.

You'll learn many things about your foe by pretending as if you are his friend. You can then use the information later on to threaten him. It is also possible to find out the things that are important to him, so you can pursue it in the future. If he tells you what he truly wants in life, you'll be able to determine what you can do to earn his full confidence so you can really destroy him. However being kind allows you to gain access to your adversaries' most vulnerable position. Once you're there, you'll be able make the biggest damage most quickly.

Betrayal deeply hurts. If you let your adversaries consider you an ally, you could hurt him more than you normally would in the sense of sabotaging him. Friendships and family members are able to inflict the worst hurts.

Make a sacrifice to the Plum Tree in order to protect the Peach Tree

Sometimes, it's best to let go of any short-term goals in order to make room to pursue a longer-term goal. Certain things aren't as crucial as your ultimate final goal, therefore they are best to forget and put aside. For example, if, for instance, you are trying to damage the reputation of someone else, but have lost credibility through the outrageous claims you make, stop the plot to safeguard your reputation. In this way, you'll be more convincing and you will keep convincing people about the facts regarding the person you are trying to hurt later.

There's a pretty brutal historical background to this strategy. The army of Cao Cao began to be starved of food throughout the Three Kingdoms Period. The army captain was instructed by Cao Cao to stretch the food supply by diluting rice by adding water. When the soldiers started to beg and complain, Cao Cao had the army captain killed. He then claimed to the world that the captain was selling the rice for the enemies. The troops were inflamed by renewed anger at the enemy and started to fight more vigorously, even the fact that their diet was struggling.

Use the opportunity for Pilfer the Goat

Profit from every little possibility or chance. Every opportunity is a chance to provide you with a the benefit. If your adversary displays an area of weakness, make the most of it quickly. Be flexible in your approach to profit from opportunities.

Get the Snake moving by hitting the grass around it

It is not a good idea to disclose your plans or your plan. If you do this you are giving your adversaries the chance to plan to take on you. Don't tell anyone what you are planning to do because you don't know who is your true partner and who's trying to harm you because they are intimate with you. Be careful about what you say to others.

In this way, you get the benefit of surprise. You could surprise your adversaries by launching an attack without warning or even betrayal.

Then, borrow another's corpse in order to revive the Soul

As a corpse would, certain old technologies, customs or concepts are gone. You can use them to come up with a fresh method of attack that your adversary isn't prepared for.

Letters are mostly obsolete. It is possible to use letters to make your enemies feel uncomfortable or to send him propaganda images. What you think is an attractive letter or card from a close friend is nothing more than a type of propaganda. It is possible to use friendly methods to disseminate ideas and fake information that can create fear among people, or cause them to take certain actions.

Make the Tiger leave its Mountain Lair

A lot of people are protected due to their position. An excellent example is when an individual is secure and secure from threats by his circle of friends or status as an authority figure. If you want to attack him, you have to draw him out of his safe zone. He is then at risk.

This is a usual tactic employed by child molesters and murderers. They know that removing someone from their life is the most effective way to break their defenses. It is possible to use this for your benefit by separating the person away from his family and friends to reduce his mental strength. He'll have less incentive to confront against you and will be more susceptible to the accusations you make. For instance, if claim that someone is not attractive around his friends and they defend them and convince him that he's beautiful. However, if you say that you're on your own and nobody else is able to stand against him then he's most likely to believe your words. Influence of suggestions is better when you're in a room by themselves.

In order to capture the Image, one must let loose

If you cause someone to feel like they are trapped in a deal or any other type of prison, the person is determined to get out. He will invest all his effort in escaping from the contract and running away further, farther away. He won't fight with for you when he is trying to get away. You can get the fight out of someone providing a glimpse of the possibility of escape. If that glimmer appears to be fake Your adversary will typically quit in despair. Your enemy is trapped.

Utilize the false promise of freedom to break the morale and despair.

The Brick is being tossed out to collect the Jade

Give your adversaries the promise of fame, money or sex. These are big temptations which almost all people take advantage of. If you offer this offer to your adversaries you are offering him a lure. If he does take the bait, he's being lured to your fate. You are now in control, and your adversary has a debt to you to compensate in exchange for the lure you provided him.

Make promises of something wonderful to convince your adversary to take action to help you. For example, if you would like a bouncer to allow you into a club you could give a financial incentive. Bouncers often are underpaid, and they will gladly accept extra money. You can influence people to gain influence over them by telling them what you really would like.

The proverb is derived from an amusing story. There was an artist named Chang Jian, who was looking to learn from the great writer, Zhao Gue. He learned about the fact that Zhao Gue would be at the local temple and so he visited the temple and composed two lines of a four-line poem that was hung on the walls. The master poet was there the temple, the unfinished poem annoyed him, so he rewrote the lines that were missing. After this Chang Jian had the opportunity gain knowledge about poetry from an expert. He got the master to stop instructing him by giving him the chance to write the poem and displaying his talents before the crowd.

Destroy the Enemy by capturing the Chief

Every person needs leaders. A leader provides guidance, motivation and encouragement. If the leader leaves the group will slide into chaos. They won't be able fight and they'll probably give up. It is possible to profit from the chaos to gain victory.

You can snare the leader in real-life by defying his image or forcing him to quit an executive position. In the event that you disable the leader his followers, they will be impervious. The likelihood is that his group will break up.

Take out the Firewood in the Cooking Pan

When you remove someone's source for strength, you could make him weaker. Like removing the firewood from the forest there will be nothing to sustain his power. You can disable your enemy by removing his supporters. Take away the people who support him. Take away his pride and self-esteem. Take away his perception of reality. Utilizing various manipulative strategies that will be covered in the future it is possible to completely disable his. Smear and isolation campaigns could help to cut off the social support he receives, while gaslighting and torture could take away the ability to think and self-assurance of his mind.

Find a Fish when the water is agitated

The use of disorientation to weaken the adversaries is an effective method of weakening his defenses. It is possible to use the most inexplicably bizarre and unexpected actions to disrupt your adversaries mental processes and render him vulnerable. Make deliberate mischief to make people lose their ability to think and the capability for self-defense.

Slough the shell of the Cicada off

There will be moments where you are in the midst of losing. In these instances, you should make it appear as if you're surrendering and surrendering. In the meantime, you can plan a sneaky attack. Your opponent will relax and believe that he has was victorious, and that's when you are able to take your next move.

It's always a good suggestion to not let the adversaries be a bit giddy. He will think that he has won. This may be a sting to the pride of yours, however it will allow him to relax. You are then guaranteed to prevail.

Shut the Door to catch the Thief

It's a fantastic strategy to completely eliminate your adversaries if you are able to. If you have knowledge or something that could completely hinder your adversaries, make use of it. Stop the war in a single, decisive step. Don't be afraid to speak up or allow your feelings to take over your life.

It's an excellent idea to abandon any pretenses of friendship or kindness when you are certain that you have the ability to win the battle. You should however, only wish to do this if you're certain that your plan is certain to be successful. Don't hesitate to give your opponent time to gather his powers. You must attack right away and go as cruel as possible.

Begin to befriend the Distant State, while attacking the Neighbor

The people who interact closely with you tend to be those you are most at war with. The people who are farther from you are often more favorable allies. Pay attention to the people you're close to and don't be a fool to them. While you're at it, figure out the people who are your friends. They may be individuals who aren't as close as you. Make use of them against your foes. Build a strong group of allies you can count on in times of you require them. Rely on the people who serve as your satellites instead of those you rely on.

This is particularly helpful in the case of mental warfare at work. People you work closely with are the ones that you depend on most. They are therefore likely to cause harm by failing to meet your expectations. Don't trust them, and make sure you are supported by other colleagues, in case those who you are close to become hostile towards you.

Get a Safe Passage to Overcome Guo's State Guo

Get the information, or other resources of an allies to fight your opponent. Use those resources to attack your person you obtained the information or resources from. This helps you stay ahead of the rest. You'll be the ultimate winner of all by not giving anyone an opportunity to get a break.

This is a reference to Chinese historical events, in which one of the military leaders took advantage of Guo's state offer of safe passage to get back at Guo and defeat it. This is the definition of betrayal, and it's not nice however, psychological warfare isn't meant to be pleasant.

Replace the Beams with Rotten Timbers

This is a simple procedure. Replace the beams, or primary supports, of your foe. Change their method of doing things to the point that they are unable to function properly. This can be done by disrupting their schedule or by removing items they depend on for their support for their livelihood, like an employment. It is possible to replace someone's wood with rotten wood , by getting their job terminated or removing any of their support systems in life. Don't underestimate the fact that people depend on routine and habits to provide support. When you take away the things that give their lives purpose and structure They are left helpless and fragile. It is then easy to destroy them.

Make a point towards the Mulberry Tree while cursing the Locust Tree

Don't name people or make obvious tips when talking to others, especially those you are fighting. Keep even your most trusted allies at a safe distance. Employ subterfuge when sharing details. This will protect you from any future liability, and lets you alter the truth in any manner that is possible.

It is best to ensure that everyone is kept on a strictly confidential basis. There is no need to make everything available to everyone. If you are able to keep things private, you will quickly control the situation. Others will act in a false assumption that they have learned from the limited information you provide. It is easy to influence circumstances by sharing only a few details. In addition, you have the ability to limit the influence of others since you are aware of something they don't.

Play Dumb

The old fashioned method. When you convince people that you're stupid it can cause them to think that you are stupid. They'll prepare themselves to attack and leave themselves vulnerable since they believe that you're too dumb to take a risk. They are not ready for the moment you come out of the shadows with an enthralling attack.

Your talent is a essential detail that you need to know and remain private about. Everyone will think that you're stupid. This way, you'll be able to emerge at the most unexpected times and take on your foes whenever you have to. This can be a sour pill to your pride , and it could be hard to fake stupidity However, it's helpful at the end of the day.

Lift the Ladder after the enemy has ascended the Roof

It's possible to get someone in the situation in which he has no support or friends. And then, let him go back to his home in order to be safe. This way you place him in a vulnerable position and vulnerable. In essence, you're placing someone in a position in which he is not protected.

It can be done in a physical or metaphorical way. Physically, you could lure an individual to a spot that he doesn't have any allies. You can then slash the tires of the car, leaving him without a home. You will be unable to defend him and you'll have absolute power over him. He might have to ask for your forgiveness to return home safely. It is possible to take advantage of his vulnerability to gain an opportunity to force him to do what you would like to get his assistance.

Metaphorically You can cause a person to feel uncomfortable by removing the entire group of acquaintances. Make it seem like life is difficult for him. Soon, he'll be asking for mercy, and you could use this circumstances for your benefit.

Deck the tree with fake Blossoms

As fake flowers can make a dead tree appear healthy and look healthy, you can also make everything look exactly as you want to. Through deceit and deceit you can make your adversaries feel uneasy about something that is harmless or think that something insignificant can be a useful tool. You can influence someone's perception by presenting falsehoods.

The psychological warfare strategy involves creating false reality for your foes. This is done through propaganda, fake news as well as other ways. Inducing your adversary to believe that something harmless is not to be taken seriously can make him with fear about absolutely nothing.

If, for instance, you have a colleague who is your enemy and your company is given an entirely manager who is new, then you may be able to convince your colleague to believe that your boss will be removing people and that their job is in danger. He'll be terrified of the new boss as well as the possibility that he could lose his job without reason. He may even quit.

It is also possible to make someone ridicule himself. Make him believe that a beautiful girl is over him. Make sure you point out the way she looks at him or the way she positions herself. This will make him want to chase her. He'll be shot and his ego will be damaged.

Create a Host and Guest Exchange roles

Make yourself appear to be someone's most beloved friend. In this means that the person allows you in. This is an opportunity to gain access within his heart to penetrate the person and then defeat him. Doing a nice job and pretending to be surrendered is a common technique to poke someone in the back.

Friendships can be used to get information about someone. Friends talk. He'll be able to relax and share important information about himself, including what he's most worried about and about what he worries the most.

This could be used as information to harm him later. Additionally, he may take you in with his loved ones. Learn how to reach his loved family members to harm him. You can convince him to believe in you for work assignments only to fail and blame the failure on you to get him in troubles at work. You can adjust your approach to friendship according to the circumstances and you'll have great results.

The Honey Trap

Utilize sexual seduction to convince people to commit a blunder or cause discord in the life of a person. You could attempt to lure someone to you or even employ a beautiful woman to take care of the task for you. Whatever you choose, you can utilize sexual intimacy to make your opponent to commit a number of mistakes.

A majority of people are intolerant to sexuality, especially when it can boost their ego. So this honey trick is certain to succeed. It is possible to get your adversaries to commit a variety of sins to have sexual sex. You can make him weaker with the promise of sexual sex with a beautiful person.

Strategies for the Empty Fort Strategy

If you feel your odds of winning are slim, then pretend you're not interested in combat in the slightest. Play it cool and calm. Your adversaries will lower their guard and assume that you are not causing harm. Your presence will no longer appear to be a threat. So, you can unleash an attack in his head in case he's not prepared for it. An element of surprise will dramatically increase your chances of winning.

Let the enemy's own spy create discord inside the Enemy Camp

By framing and rumors by framing and rumors, you can cause someone to appear unlikable to their loved ones, their family, friends and others who love them. This could cause conflict between your adversaries and their family members. It could disrupt the support system of his family and create a mess for him. Use only convincing evidence to discredit an individual's appearance before their family members.

Risk self-harm to gain the Trust of the enemy

Try to pretend that you've harm yourself. The people will think you're not dangerous and you are able to be taken seriously. They'll feel bad for you, and they will relax in their attempts to help you. This is the time to be cobras.

You could also claim that your injury was caused by an opponent which you and your adversary have in common. Then, both of you appear to be in a state of collusion. Your adversaries will assume that you're an ally in order to retaliate against the enemy you share. However, in reality, you're not allies with any person.

Combine Strategies

Do not be afraid to combine strategies. The more strategies you apply the more likely your success is. Combining tactics is a fantastic method of provoking and battering people mentally. Utilize all these strategies at once to batter someone and one after the other to reduce his defenses. Don't be afraid to unleash numerous attacks. This can boost your chances of winning.

If All Other Options Fail If All Other Options Fail, Resign

It is important to know when to quit before you're destroyed. Certain people are impossible to be broken. If you find that psychological warfare is creating damage that isn't worth it, think about resigning. It's not easy to let go but it could help you at the final.

When you have given up it doesn't mean the fight will never end. It is possible to start an attack again later in the event that your opponent is least likely to be expecting it.

Additional Psychological Warfare Methods

Primary Objectives

The main objectives in this war on the mind is the reputation as well as the mind. Focus more on these targets more than anything else. When you hit these areas, it will can defeat your adversaries and win the battle.

When you do harm to someone's reputation, you do a lot of amazing things. In one way, you could make the person appear to be a shady person to the world at large. The validity of their actions could be questioned. Therefore, a person is in your hands. You can do whatever you want but he or she can't convince anyone else that they're in danger. Additionally, by causing harm to the reputation of a person, you cause people feel be hurt. You take away the prestige of their work, and even credibility. Others will disliking the victim.

The mind is your next next target. If you break the victim's brain you create his emotional distress and discomfort. You make him be skeptical of himself or harm himself in a bid to remove your influence. In the end, your victim may end up ruining his life to benefit you. It is not necessary to do anything at all to harm your victim. The benefit of mental warfare is it will take care of all the work. It's all you have to do is hurt his mind, which renders him unfit to fight and think clear.

Know Your Enemy Well

Make sure you know your opponent thoroughly. This shouldn't be too difficult, as most of your enemies are those you have once loved dearly. If you don't know your adversaries well You must become acquainted with them. You can do this in any way required.

Understanding the things that scare your enemy is the most crucial thing you should know to be able to use psychological warfare. Psychological warfare is effective when it is employed to create tension and heighten the terror of your adversaries.

Lower Intelligence

J.F.C. Fuller predicted that the government would participate in the gradual lowering of society through reducing the amount of education offered. In the end, the population would be more susceptible to the influence of propaganda as they do not be able to reason or think rationally. You can make use of this to your advantage by making your fellow citizens feel stupid. You can appear to have more intelligence than them and they can't possibly comprehend the way you think. If people feel stupid they're more likely accept your word as truth.

Propaganda

It is a highly effective method of demoralizing and overcoming adversaries. It is possible to propagate ideas and feelings like fear. It is also employed to create mass of hysteria. If you are using it for personal purposes the idea of spreading propaganda to communities or even individuals to get people to believe in a concept that you would like them to be convinced of.

Propaganda can take different forms. Flyers, newspaper ads, as well as email messages are all effective ways to disseminate propaganda. It is easy to disseminate ideas of propaganda. For example as part of an experiment in social media the myth that people eat eight spiders every year when they sleep was published on the internet. This was quickly re-circulated as factual information, and today this misconception is now common known. Many believe that humans actually devour eight spiders each year during their sleeping.

Make posts that are highly credible and write them in boldness and authority. It is possible to claim that the posts or messages come from higher authority or a fake government agency. You'll be amazed at by how many people accept the information as factual when it is authoritative to it. A majority of people accept the facts they hear and do not do further investigation or ask questions.

The power of propaganda is not always working for everyone. Certain people may have questions or raise doubts. But if you are able to convince the person or group you want to target to believe in what you are saying and believe in your message, then you have done very well. You've influenced the thinking of some key people through your messages.

It is important to teach individuals to be informants so that they are willing to expose themselves to propaganda on their own volition. Make use of positive reinforcement to entice those who request details. This will ensure that they remain relying on you as a reliable source for news. You will be able to shape the information they receive from the world outside and influence the way they think.

Learninged the importance of helplessness

The study of learnt helplessness has shown how powerful this psychological force has on animals and humans alike. When someone learns that their best efforts are in vain as fighting will only make it worse, he / will quit. They will depend on others to help giving up the freedom to others. However, even if the situation is changed the person will remain in a state of helplessness since it's an acquired behavior and a way of dealing with all aspects of life that they have acquired.

A well-known experiment on dogs known as The Learned Helplessness Study illustrates this fact. The study was conducted by researchers Mark Seligman and Steve Maier conducted this study on dogs in the year 1965. They placed three distinct groups of dogs into harnesses. The first group was let out of the harness after a couple of hours, with no damage done to the dogs. The second group was split into pairs, tied together before being given a shock that was administered by a tiny electric shock coming from an apparatus that can be stopped with a press the lever. Dogs from the 3rd group joined together, and one dog was shocked, however press the lever in the device didn't cause any change to stop the shocks.

Then, all the dogs of the three groups were put into an enclosure. They were given shocks randomly while inside the box. The dogs were able to escape these shocks by jumping out of the door of the box. The dogs of the groups 1 and 2 leapt into the boxes right away to escape the pain caused by the shocks. The dogs of Group 3 however, were conditioned to remain helpless and put their feet in the box believing that there was nothing they could do to avoid the pain of the shocks. The group 3 dogs learned to leap out of the box after they were physically pushed out by the scientists at minimum twice. They were required to be taught how to get out of their suffering.

This study suggests that animals, and consequently peoplecan be taught to feel ineffective. If they believe that nothing could be done to prevent an unfortunate situation, they get complacent and will not take action even though a simple solution is right in front of their eyes. The people who become powerless are reliant on a person else to assist them in learning how to conquer their problems.

If your patient is unable to get away from your specific method of torture, you can help them learn helplessness. It is possible to use the concept of learned helplessness to control your victim. You could also employ it to get your victim to abandon the fight. Your victim will then become an ally of yours, which puts you in total control and control.

Discreditation

Discreditation is the act of taking someone's credibility away. It can be done by many ways. There are a variety of methods to accomplish this. Internet and slander are utilized to destroy the reputation of the victim in opinions of other people. The lack of sleep and manipulation of emotions can cause the victim to create a negative impression and make them appear insane.

The best way to discredit someone is through collaboration between a number of individuals. They can appear as if they don't care and do not have any personal involvement in the battle. They might be people in positions of power like police officers, judges, and mortgage lenders. As if they are uninterested as a third-party, they could be able to impose harsh judgments on anyone. Their opinions can cause a person to question the reason they appear so reprehensible and untrustworthy to others. It can damage a person's trustworthiness and credibility.

The discrediting of someone's reputation can be devastating in the eyes of the public. However, it also erodes the person's self-esteem. The victim starts to doubt the truth of the truth when all evidence seems to be in contradiction with what he or perceives. For example, if he perceives a conflict in one direction, however an official who is involved in the manipulation exposes that the situation went quite differently, the victim may be unsure of what the truth really is. They will live in a state of doubt, where it is easy to be deceived. Then, it's easy to cause harm to the victim.

Self-destruction

It is simple to employ psychological warfare to force people into self-destruct. Because of desperation and despair some people may attempt to hurt himself or herself as a result of psychological combat. Most often, they be sent to a psych prison or a psych you will not be convicted of assault. However, you may have been in a position to induce people to self-harm.

If you are relentless and uncompromising By being relentless and merciless, you make your victim believe that they can't remove your ruthless and uncompromising behavior. If nobody else is convinced of the claims of psychological torture, you will be in a bind and will feel that the person is going mad. Therefore, he or she might try to kill himfor herself in order to rid themselves of the feeling of being insane. They may decide that cutting themselves is the best method to rid yourself of you. If they are not able to die and living, then the life of that person is basically over. Due to lawful suicide, the loved one could be locked up and his or her credibility will be further eroded.

It can result in the need for homelessness and poverty when the person is released from an institution. The person now is considered insane and may be diagnosed as having a mental disorder. This makes obtaining work and integrating to society a challenge. Additionally, you could increase your efforts in the field of psychology to bring the person's sanity even more. The person is likely to be insane at this point , and completely cannot function as a normal citizen of society.

You have totally damaged the life of someone. They've been driven to self-harm , or the death penalty or poverty or homelessness. They aren't able to have the things they once had.

Grid Awareness

Grid awareness refers to the network of people who are aware of the psychological combat. They might suspect or be aware there is a psychological war being carried out on them. They may have similar suspicions and they may share opinions like, "No one wants me to be aware of this. I could be into serious trouble if openly talk regarding it."

Grid awareness is a naive indicator that allows the majority of people to recognize the fact that mental warfare real and is occurring to them. It's proof that psychological warfare is real and is actually working. If you are unsure exploring the web and blogs that are dedicated to the subject of psychological warfare will reveal how many people have eerily similar experiences about their own. Although they don't understand who's responsible for the war but they usually conclude that it's their neighbors or family members or even those from the CIA or NSA.

However, grid awareness is a danger for those using these techniques. Although you might not be discovered but grid awareness could be problems. The possibility of people slipping out of your grasp should you ever be found out. They'll immediately become defensive and will try to stop you from trying to manage them. It is essential to take measures to avoid this awareness becoming a mass hysteria, or real knowledge. It's one of the best ways to keep grid awareness from revealing your secret operation.

The first step is to be alert for any signs of awareness among your victims. Follow their social media accounts and blogs, if they've got blogs. Also , observe their behaviour. Are they becoming more cautious and suspicious, hostile or perhaps outwardly defensive and hostile? Rapid changes in their behavior could indicate that they're beginning to think they are a threat to you.

It is then time to put off fighting for a period of time. This is merely temporary interruption to your operations. You'll be able to resume it in the future. At the moment, you'd like to be careful not to confirm anyone's suspicions. Keep your manners professional and courteous and refrain from engaging in any unusual behaviour. It is important to avoid changing your usual manners However, don't stop doing the things you usually do. Simply approach your victims with any ulterior motives for a short time.

Do your best try to convince your victim feel as if they're crazy. Use manipulation to convince them that they're crazy and that you're free of any accusations. In fact, make them doubt your sanity by pointing out the other things they're not or by proving the degree of innocence and goodness you are. Psychological warfare is not new and a lot of people don't even know that it could occur to them. There's always a tinge of uncertainty in relation to grid awareness. Use that doubt to your advantage. You can also take advantage of the fact that there's no evidence to support your claim.

Reputation and reputations of the people you are discrediting If you have to. You don't want anyone else to believe what they're telling the world. Of course, the majority of people have found claims of mental mind control difficult to believe, and you'll have an advantage your defense. The majority of people are already inclined to doubt and deny the claims of your clients. They'll assume that your victims are suffering from schizophrenia that they are paranoid. However, there will always be some people who could be in agreement with their statements and believe what they're declaring. It is possible to increase security by sharing information that you have obtained for example, via the Internet which will destroy and damage your victim's reputations. It is also possible to make them appear as if they are fools on the street, ruining their public image. In the ideal scenario, you'll perform this before you start the psychological warfare.

By following these guidelines it is possible to shield yourself from being found out. It is vital to ensure that you don't become a target. However, the chance of getting arrested is extremely small. Psychological warfare is usually invisible to the majority of people. Also, it is unlikely to reveal any clues or provide any evidence. Only you will be able to comprehend your motives as well as what you're up to, which means you are more likely than others to never discover your activities. Even suspicion is a possibility to be dismissed and then destroyed.

Ideas for Planting

The exposure to ideas could cause your adversaries to accept these concepts. When they become real and your adversaries are less likely to challenge them.

Hitler as well as other political leaders have a reputation for using the media, including plays, to expose people to certain vile concepts. Hitler utilized the most disturbing plays to implant thoughts into people's minds. German populace. After watching a play that was disturbing for instance, the audience would be unable to comprehend. There was no harm to them from the ideas by the drama, and so they concluded that there was nothing wrong with these concepts. When Hitler was able to present this idea to military personnel, not one expressed concern.

This can be used for your own psychological warfare. Inflict fear on people by imagining conversations, Youtube movies, TV programs or other forms of media. People will begin to accept the notions as harmless. They will not be able to fight so much after you make the concepts a actual.

Chapter 3: Psychological Torture

Psychological torture is important to understand. Torture is a constant result, or an elemental part of fighting. Since the beginning of warfare in the human race, individuals have employed torture on opponents to make them weaker. It is a great way to gain information and can be a great way to degrade someone's mental state.

While you're unlikely to find someone gagged and bound inside your secret underground dungeon, for the purpose of torture knowing how to break the mind will give you some useful suggestions to use psychological combat. There are methods to use techniques like the use of sensory overload in order to make your adversaries get a frenzied.

In addition, if you encounter someone who is bound to the ground in your underground cavern you'll know what you need to do. While physical punishment is not the best idea, there could be circumstances in your life that could actually apply it. Make sure you are aware that the law does not permit torture. It's also not always needed for personal use of psychological warfare.

Psychological torture can employ physical methods to harm the mind of an adversary. However, psychological methods of torture are focused on destroying the human mind and causing mental harm to someone. By using humiliation, fear, and manipulating the sensory system it is possible to cause someone to break. It can make him doubt his ability to see reality and undermine his self-confidence. You could also force someone to do whatever you wish to get rid of the terrible emotions that you're causing him.

A variety of these techniques of torture are used by the CIA as well as the Department of Defense on political prisoners. They are tried and tested methods of bribing prisoners into confessing. They can also be very effective to disable your adversaries' mental strength and mental sanity. When you make someone insane it is possible to harm them, denigrate them, and eliminate them as potential threats to your war efforts. Once I've covered these techniques, I'll give you some realistic variations of torture suitable for home usage. You are able to adapt these methods to your own needs however you like. One of the advantages of the act of torture is that it is fun to use.

Common Torture Methods

Sensory Deprivation

Sensory deprivation is the reason for one or more of the person's senses to be totally removed. All stimulation to this particular sense is cut off. It is possible to remove someone's sight or hearing, or sensation of touching. The deprivation of stimulation for all the senses can work effectively. It is possible to shut off all of an individual's senses, thereby destroying his sense of sanity as well as his understanding of life.

The human brain needs stimulation through sensory stimuli to keep its perspective of the world and perception of reality. The absence of the glimpses of reality that are provided by the sensory organs may cause it lose ability to perceive and ability to comprehend. The brain is prone to hallucinations and confusion while it attempts to produce sensory stimulation and a sense of reality in order to make up for the reality that is not there. Sometimes, the loss of reality can be permanent. It is possible to permanently damage people's mental health by denying them sensory stimulation. They'll never be same, as the many victims of this sort of suffering can attest to.

The monotony of sensory stimulation may be a similar effect as deprivation of sensory input. A monotone sound or stimulation that is constant and static causes what's commonly referred to as"the "ganzfeld effects." This result is the same as the effects of deprivation in sensory perception. The human brain is not able to cope with listening or seeing exact stimulus for long enough. This could lead to a complete concentration on the stimulus that is the same thing as sensory loss.

To show how severe sensory deprivation can be an issue, let's take a virtual tour of an area that's called the most quiet space in existence. This room is situated at Orfield Laboratories. Orfield Laboratories in Minneapolis, Minnesota. It's ninety-nine percent sound-absorbing and is the quietest human-made structure on the planet. It is impossible to remain in the room for more than 45 minutes. The mere act of being within the space for a prolonged duration of time can trigger bizarre hallucinations. If you make prisoners to remain in a prison for more than 45 minutes, you could end his life.

Sensory Overload

Sensory over stimulation is exactly the opposite of deprivation of sensory stimulation, and it performs exactly the same way. When you expose someone to excessive stimulation in any one of their senses could cause sensory overload. It is possible to bombard someone with too much sound as well as strobe lights, or other stimulation to make them insane. In fact, overloading their senses is particularly powerful.

Sensory overload causes people to feel angry, depressed and overwhelmed in a short time. They'll find it difficult to concentrate and may be easily annoyed, even when they are exposed to physical stimulation like the clothes they wear. They might become deranged and become violent even towards themselves. A prolonged exposure could lead to hallucinations and post-traumatic stress disorders an ongoing reaction to trauma.

There is a belief that the inhabitants of cities are afflicted with a mild type of sensory oversaturation. It causes people living in cities to be more stressed and angry than those who live in more tranquil surroundings.

Sleep Deprivation

The negative effects of sleeping deprivation were made public through a publicity stunt in 1959 in which an Top 40 radio personality named Peter Tripp challenged himself to endure two hundred hours of sleeping for two hundred hours. The goal of the stunt was to raise money for people who participated in March of Dimes, but it eventually revealed the consequences of sleep deprivation to the human brain. After a short period of remaining alert, Tripp began to hallucinate after forty hours. By the time he reached that point the man required help from chemicals to stay awake and functioning. Although Tripp was not afflicted with permanent injury due to the "Wake-a-Thon," he made evident how dangerous a sleeping less can be. Other people who tried (sometimes successful) in achieving his feat, for instance students at high schools like Randy Gardner who made it two hundred and sixty-four consecutive hours awake and experienced hallucinations too. The psychosis that is associated with the use of stimulants is largely caused by sleeping deprivation.

Due to its destructive effects on the human brain sleep deprivation can be an effective psychological torture technique. By preventing someone from sleeping by disrupting their attempts to fall asleep or by administering stimulants like amphetamines can mentally destabilize the individual. After a period of time the person will start to experience hallucinations and may not be able maintain their perception of the reality.

Mock Executions

The staging of the execution of someone can cause extreme terror that can cause a person to break. One could be led to believe that they are being manipulated into the execution of himself or be ordered to watch an execution faked by someone he cherishes or a fellow prisoner in his motive. Watching someone die or thinking that he's going to die can cause someone to scream in terror. He may even utter a desired confession.

Humans are programmed to be apathetic at the thought of hurt to another human being. The way to induce hysteria is someone by exposing them to the death of another even if the death is fake. It is possible to cause the person to lose control of himself and become terrified.

White Torture

White torture is a combination of sensory deprivation with isolation, resulting in the perfect method of torture. People are usually incapable of enduring any form of torture for long, before they lose their identity or even how to socialize. The harm is usually permanent.

White torture is usually conducted in a setting that is completely white. White walls, furniture made of white, or even rice that is served in white plates. Prisoners are only able to see white. Britain is known to make use of white noise, too. This lack of stimulation can trigger the "eld effect" that I mentioned earlier.

A survivor of white torture who explains the long-term impact that white torture has caused to its mental wellbeing. He can't rest without taking sedatives. And it is still lonely, even decades later. He feels so lonely due to the fact that the person he is with doesn't feel comfortable with himself, or engage in conversations or relationships with others.

The awe and pain that white torture can cause often can lead to victims and prisoners confessing. Even if they're not guilty, some people confess to crimes to get away from the mind-numbing isolation and the horror of torture in white.

Chinese Water Torture

Chinese water torture also referred to by the name of Spanish water torture is an type of torture in which water is dripped on the skin of a person to cause anxiety and psychosis. Humans are taught by experience that water makes hollows in the ground therefore they believe that the constant drip of water will create a hollow in their forehead. The stimulation from the dripping water can be very repetitive, which can lead to sensory overstimulation. Both of these emotions could cause great pain among the victims.

Waterboarding

Waterboarding is a simulation of drowning. The person is strapped to an inflatable board with his head in the direction of his face before being submerged in water, or water is poured over the air passages. The brief feeling of drowning is so uncomfortable that it can occasionally cause people to cry and admit to the interrogation. Fear of death as well as the desire to escape from the uncomfortable circumstances could cause victims to break down in order to get away.

Hooding

Hooding means covering a person's head with an opaque, dark hood. The victim is unaware of what's happening to him and his breath, sight, and breath are being restricted. The victim will experience a sense of anxiety and fear. It can be helpful to make a fake attack or assault other prisoners around him in order to make him think that he's about to be assaulted. Hooding is also employed against prisoners who will soon be hanged or executed. This can increase the fear of their execution and increases the fear of death the prisoners already feel.

Half-Hanging

Half-hanging is the process of securing the rope around a victim's neck until he dies from deprivation of oxygen. The patient is revived, and the process repeated. The fear of deprivation of oxygen is instinctual and natural to all. In addition, the constant lack of oxygen may have detrimental consequences for the brain of a person. Thus, those who do not have oxygen is most likely to admit. The victims will want to stop the half-hanging as quickly as possible, and this will lead them to admit to the crime.

Walling

Walling refers to the process whereby subjects are equipped with an arm. They are repeatedly pushed against walls by the collar. They bounce off the wall due to their shoulders and only suffer minor bruising. Most often, only a rubber wall is employed. This is due to the fact that physical injury isn't the primary goal of this type of torture. The sensation of being tossed around can be frightening and even dizzying. It can cause prisoners to break. This gives the torturer absolute control.

Electric Shock Torture

Although electric shocks are physical, it can cause an atmosphere of fear and shame in the victims. When the pain and discomfort of electric shocks intensify, people typically lose control of their bladders and bowels. This can cause them to feel humiliated and suffering.

They're more likely to collapse and confess when an electrical shocks are administered.

Parrilla is an form of electric shock torture which involves connecting people to a grill that is made of steel and then burning them with electric current. Most often, electrodes are connected around the victim's nose as well as temples and genitalia. These are the most sensitive areas of the body. Parrilla can be uncomfortable and embarrassing.

Nuremburg Plate

The most popular use of the device was during the medieval times and it is believed that the Nuremburg Plate is a massive torment device that resembles a Merry-Go-Round and is designed to resemble an elongated wheel. Subjects are tethered to the plate with their legs and arms and then spin in a circular motion. The spinning causes dizziness, disorientation, and nausea in the patients. It's extremely uncomfortable and makes the victim feel helpless.

Nuremburg Plate Nuremburg Plate was used only in it's Nuremburg Castle in Bavaria, Germany. It is believed that it was never utilized in any other context than Nuremburg

Castle. It was often used to punish the king's perpetrators, who were accused of being treasonous.

Starvation

It can mean refusing to eat or telling prisoners that the food he eats is poisoned, so that he'll not eat the food or to throw it away. Although the human body is able to endure for a long time without food, starvation may cause people to become depressed and insane. They often admit to or give in to the temptation of eating. They can't retain their mental faculties long when they are severely malnourished.

The use of starvation has been how many were able to occupy opponents or stop attacks. It's also used to deal with POWs. In the event of starving someone, it becomes an endurance race between the person's willpower and your patience. If your patience is insatiable and you can be a slave to someone until he falls.

Feathering and Tarring

The use of feathers and tarring was used to sever prisoners. They would be taken captive then smothered in tar and then wrapped in feathers. The feathers and the tar would make people uncomfortable. However, the true punishment was the humiliation the victims were then subjected to while they were forced to perform in the public. People would often yell at them and throw objects at them. The jeering of the public created an awful psychological trauma for those who suffered from feathering and tarring.

Bamboo Torture

Bamboo torture was a popular method of torture throughout Asia during WWII during the war, when soldiers were shackled and suspended from the bushes of bamboo. Bamboo is a fast-growing plant and incredibly fast-growing, it was just a matter of time until the young shoots got tall enough to cut through the prisoners body. Bamboo shoots are extremely sharp and caused immense pain, and sometimes even death on prisoners. The psychological component of this torture lies in prisoners were required to hang on the ground for days in anticipation of slow, unavoidable discomfort. Sometimes , they'd surrender before the bamboo was able to penetrate them.

Abacination

Abacination involves slowly blinding someone over time. By using a chemical drip that destroys the eye's tissues, prisoners have to remain in the dark and endure an ever-increasing loss in vision. As the darkness of the world increases over them, they usually fall down and confess in a state of shock. It is possible to make someone insane for a long time through traumatizing them.

Making Torture more suitable for home use

A lot of these techniques of torture are not suitable to use on a personal basis. It is not possible to use these types of torture without being detected. It is possible to be charged for assault if discovered to be employing these methods. You can however, use these methods of torture and adapt them to more practical at-home usage.

Based on the above concepts and you'll be able to see that causing a person to lose their senses is the best method to hurt them and cause them to doubt the reality. It's easy to use sensory loss or overload in real life , without having to work to do so. Inflicting fear on people or the threat of death works well in gaining control over them. Remember these tips when you create the personal terror techniques.

Repetition

As you can see in the last section on torture, the repetition of one stimulus could drive an individual insane. A slow drip from water, for example could cause someone to lose control, become angry, or even begin hallucinating. This can lead to self-harm, or even commit suicide.

It's not always possible to put someone in the torture chamber, and expose them constant stimulation. But , you can still be a threat their attention by providing the same stimuli in their vehicle or at home. Think about the things that make people go insane naturally. A lot of people don't like the sound of chewing their food. Dogs who lick themselves are another sound that is not acceptable to people. The sound of water dripping certainly can be harmful to people. White torture works due to the repeated use of white and the white noise. It is possible to use this knowledge to create an invincible torture device that will make anyone get insane.

You can see how fast people get aggressive when neighbors make them a mess by making repetitive noises like smashing nails into roofs or playing music with a distinct bass thump. The relationship between neighbors will soon be stressed. You can utilize this natural dislike of sound to your advantage and create an unstoppable presence if you're waging an attack on your neighbors.

The issue with this the issue is that you won't only target your neighbor whom you would like to inflict pain on, but you could affect other people. Your torture will be observed by others and that's never something you want to see when it comes to psychological warfare.

Another issue is that you could be a target for legal noise-related complaints. It's a good idea to make a continuous noisy, annoying sound, and then turn it off before police or the landlord is required to investigate. Your neighbors will inform you that the noise doesn't seem to be there. Your neighbors will be concerned that they might be insane.

You could also cause a person to become insane by installing an instrument that emits kind of high-pitched sound inside the home.

The same sound that is installed in your car will cause further stress and result in a successful torture. There are online devices which emit high-frequency sounds to deter bats. It is also possible to purchase white noise devices. These machines are typically employed in white torture, which is very effective.

A steady, low sound can be extremely powerful. Many have reported hearing hums in specific areas of the globe, such as Taos, New Mexico, and Bristol, England. These sounds are not explained and are believed to be that originate in within the Earth itself. They have no explanation from science to these hums. The hum that is so mysterious for the victim could be blamed in part on Earth noises.

There are many stories of strange noises that are driving people insane. It is just one of those sounds that frustrates and confuses those who have to listen frequently.

It is not necessary to use sound. You can use visual cues. When you expose an individual to the same stimulus repeatedly could cause irritation and possibly cause injury. Flashing lights and repeated propagandistic images can be two kinds of visual stimuli that could be monotonous. You could use something similar to disco balls to create flashing lights that could make someone insane.

Repeating the same phrase repeatedly to someone could cause them to break their minds. People can quickly get angry in the event that you continue to say the same repeated phrase repeatedly. There is no differentiation in the stimulus and the sense of insult those who repeat themselves feel has on their intellect can cause someone to go insane.

Isolation

It's not a good idea to place someone you're familiar with in the torture chamber or in a the sensory tank. However, you can separate an individual emotionally and socially especially if the person has a close relationship with you. If you are close with someone, you may gradually demand that they stops seeing his family and friends. You can make up stories and discuss past experiences that cause the person to not want to be around family and friends any more. Explain to him that he is superior to those he loves and that he doesn't have the right to how people treat him. Give him a few examples of how family members and friends caused him harm or did not respect him.

You could also create geographical distance to increase the gap in your life that you're trying to fill. Make a smart relocation to another location to keep someone from the people he loves. In time, he'll gradually stop communicating with family and acquaintances.

Also, you must stop the development of new friendships. You can accomplish this by limiting his access the world outside. Stay in a remote location and leave those who have no vehicle or means to leave. Be sure to supervise any interactions with strangers. If someone leaves your home Always be present and control conversations so that they can't talk to others. As time passes, you'll begin to make him fearful of the world outside by telling him stories about the horrible people that exist and how frightening the world can be. If your victim does venture out, create horrific or terrifying situations that can cause him to be scared and believe that the world is a place of the pain of being outside. Your victim will be afflicted with anxiety and will want to be inside every day, free of fear.

If you isolate an individual completely, you could reduce his social connections that help to strengthen his sense of self-worth and mental stability. You will see him disappear a bit when he is isolated. Without anyone to define who he truly is He will start to unravel at a distance. His calm will wane when he gets irrational and desperate. He'll start to believe and believe everything you say to him. He will trust your complete trust for everything.

The victims also become completely dependent on their captors to make social contact and you can utilize this advantage to your advantage. Since there is no one else to report your abuse and torture, you can get your victim to trust your complete trust. The victim will no longer have a base to guide what behavior to expect from people as a result, and he'll begin to accept your brutality and brutality as normal. He will be reliant on you for updates and advice and will be convinced that what he's doing is the right thing to do. You can tell him what you'd like him to know to make him your ideal puppet.

Threats

Threats are among the most powerful and effective methods to achieve what you want of the person you are trying to get. By making threats to someone's safety or the safety of their loved ones it is possible to gain control over his feelings and convince him to follow your wishes. It can also undermine the sense of security and reduce his sense of security. The fear you create affects his life quality very significantly.

The greatest threat to the home is not against one's physical wellbeing. It is possible to be charged with physical threats. Your threat must be directed at someone's integrity and reputation. Blackmail is a great tool to use in this case. If you're able to find relevant information about someone, which could damage their reputation, you can use it as a way to control him and force the person to perform the things you require. If you are unable to find information about someone, you can make up some reliable facts and fabricate evidence to launch a successful propaganda campaign. Inventing information is a good idea however almost everyone has dirt from their past. It is easy to gain control over someone by revealing the tiniest of details that could smear his image and make his family leave him.

It's an excellent idea to become extremely close with those whom you wish to be able to blackmail. This will increase the chance of them confiding with your or doing something shady within your circle. Begin to get acquainted with their family and their friends. Set yourself up in the most convenient place they are, so you can easily spy on their activities. Conduct a thorough investigation into their past, possibly posing as a private detective or another person to find details about them from former employers, professors, or even former classmates and friends. If you have enemies, be quiet and discretely talk to their adversaries to gather more information about their background. You'll be shocked by how eager people are to discuss their friends. The internet can provide you with many details.

In the event of a crisis you may also use threats of financial ruin or harm to loved ones or pets. But, these threats aren't as effective since you're less likely to be able to take action upon them. Blackmail is the most effective method to intimidate someone effectively.

Harassment

As of 1974 Bashir Kouchacji, a former police officer was arrested and was tortured in Beirut due to an underlying political issue. Then, he left Lebanon to establish his own restaurant, the Marrakesh Restaurant in Washington, D.C. At the point he thought that things were going well but he was greeted with numerous threatening, bizarre phone calls from his establishment in the year 1983. The calls would make threats to the restaurant owner and demand cash, and use a myriad of different voices. The calls would follow his wherever he went, at his house, at job, the Marrakesh's restaurant's sister and even the hotels in which the traveler was. When the FBI identified the calls they discovered that they came from a variety of payphones across the city. The calls were received in such a high frequency that they were often coming from multiple locations simultaneously it was evident that numerous people had to be part of the plot.

In the wake of the harassment, Kouchacji started to experience nightmares. Then, he became insane and was taken to a psychiatric institution. Since then, he's not been able to get his head around. Calls continue to come in occasionally and Kouchacji often has to go back to the hospital in order to find some rest. The constant calls have literally driven Kouchacji insane.

This story demonstrates how frequently and persistent harassment can damage people's happiness and sanity. It is easy to use aggressive harassment as a method of psychological torture and war. It is possible to use harassing phone messages, notes, emails or letters to drive people insane. It is also important to ensure that the origin of the harassing email cannot be traced to ensure that you don't get arrested and charged with harassment.

Stalking

Stalking is a type of harassment which involves the use of terror and the risk of bodily injury. Stalking can be used to scare the victim. If you pursue people and make them live their lives with terror and cause them to be afraid to turn off their lights in the evening. It creates a constant presence that takes away their peace and ability to live their lives. Being a victim of a stalker can drastically reduce the quality of life for a person and result in a lot of psychological trauma which is why it's a powerful and brutal method of psychological violence.

If you're not traceable as stalkers, you may make someone feel like they're in a state of panic. Everyone else is not going to accept that they have been harassed. The police won't assist them. But you will continue to gain absolute control over the stalkers. The majority of victims endure 100 instances of stalking before they ever even call the police. Thus, you could be able to cause a lot of damage before the possibility of legal action is even a possibility.

In one instance one teacher with special needs had a brief affair with an over-controlling pharmacist. The pharmacist started flooding her cell phone with vulgar messages and calls. He would show up at her school, then follow her home, and even knock on her door at 3 a.m. He would always appear to be monitoring her. The young lady quickly suffered from severe anxiety issues and was contemplating suicide. Her issues lasted for months after. This is a good illustration of how stalking can harm people.

One method to use the art of stalking to make your actions appear like those of a supernatural being. You could cause someone to experience intense pain while discrediting their credibility.

Gaslighting

Gaslighting will be explained in more detail in the next chapter. It is an excellent technique to make someone doubt the validity of his thinking and make him feel as if he's in a state of breakdown or is becoming insane. Gaslighting can be used as an alternative to torture and not appear as if you're doing something wrong to anyone. It is simple to use gaslighting to people you meet frequently.

To fully understand the meaning of gaslighting to understand what it is, I'll first clarify where the term originated from. It was in the 1930s that an extremely disturbing drama was released in which an abusive husband would dim the gaslights in his home to a low level. When his wife complained that the house was darker, he explained to she that his gas lighting was on normal levels and she was simply imagining the situation. Then, he began to explain to her that the people who stopped by to look into the family were only figments from her mind. She began to doubt her own mental sanity, and she fell into a shambles. She became depressed and discovered that her life was very unpleasant.

It is possible to make people doubt their own sanity by telling them that the opposite of what they believe to be factual. For instance you could tell them that it's sunny even though it's raining. In general, however, the practice of gaslighting is a lot more subtle. The gaslighter will say that someone is rewriting all the things said during the course of an exchange, for example. In constant contradiction to someone's perception of all their senses could cause them to doubt whether what they believe to be accurate. It's a method to undermine confidence in someone else.

Gaslighting is best for family members and those are often around. The isolation can help in these situations as it shields your victim from external sources to confirm that they are not in fact going mad. Social support can help someone overcome gaslighting, so restrict social contacts.

Simmering Fear

You could make someone feel very insecure by playing with their inherent fear-based instincts. If you can create anxiety in someone it can make their life miserable. However, you could also appear as if you're an obedient Good Samaritan simply watching to look out for his. Utilize the influence of suggestions to instill thoughts in the mind of someone else regarding the dangers that exists in this world. Retell stories about how unsafe the area is or how dangerous his home is. Inform him that there were people murdered in the house. This can make him feel frightened and uncomfortable, and it will make him feel fearful. You could ruin his peace at home, and cause him to be a bit frightened by anxiety.

Chapter 4: Demonic Thinking Operations And Process

In the story we talked about concerning a spirit being exiled from a house and returning to its home there are some important lessons which should not be missed. It is a glimpse into how demonic beings perceive and function.

They have the power to influence humankind both internal as well as externally.

* They travel through space (electromagnetic wave).

* They may rest after they locate a home (Neurological systems).

* They possess a sense of being. They think, think about and make decisions, as well as behave.

* They believe of their Neurological body is where they are.

* They are able to be able to communicate (communications skills)

* They have ranks that is determined by the negative effects they are taught to cause. This is the reason why the demon left its home and went to get seven other entities "eviler than it."

Never forget that, no matter how powerful these forces appear to be, they have already been defeated. You have the power to end them and take them out. Don't be afraid to exercise your authority. You are an infant and a member of God as well as your father are both one!

The Cycle of Demonic Influence Demonic Influence negative thoughts and behavior Negative behavior can lead to actions of the flesh (anger and jealousy, depression, hatred or jealousy.)

Works of the Flesh can lead to negative thinking processes. Negative thinking processes can cause physiological and psychological conditions

In the event that a person who is unbelievers has an empty home (Neurological System) and is devoid of authority due to the fact that they are not believing, this cycle will repeat itself and eventually lead to the destruction within the organism. This is a result of the degeneration and breakdown in the Immune body, Neurological system, and the Central Nervous system.

Demonic Dream Infiltration

We have all had the things we refer to as dreams. These can be positive ones like running through fields of gorgeous flowers, flying through the air and feeling the ultimate freedom or even swimming into the ocean like the most gorgeous sea mermaid. However, they can be extremely negative dreams , which are known as night terrors or nightmares. They could be actual terrifying attacks from the devil within our dreams or you could recall a terrifying event you've experienced in the past. In these nightmares, you could be murdered, stabbed or shot, or any of a myriad of other terrifying scenarios.

If we experience positive dreams typically, they cause us to awake with more positive mood. The positive experiences do not make us spend the day reminiscing about the adverse aspects in the dream. We only have positive memories of the dreams. Sometimes we laugh when recalling these dreams, and we sometimes inform our family and friends about the dream either in their lightheartedness or beauty. When we do experience nightmares, when we feel distressed after experiencing them and we recall all the negative elements of the nightmare. It is possible to be a bit frightened by the memory of what transpired in that nightmare.

The horrors of the night can cause feelings of loneliness, anger, depression and anxiety, fear, and many other feelings which are negative in nature. A large number of people suffering from mental disorders experience nightmarish nightmares regularly. Many suffer from anxiety attacks when they are trying to get to sleep due to the fear of experiencing a nightmare again. In the night, those who are experiencing nightmares may cry out to get help, or shout out due to the anxiety of the experience, or gasp when they awake from the nightmare.

The enemy can influence our thoughts, not just during the daytime, but also when our minds are dream state. The person who believes is not in any way immune to this. Any thoughts that we let rule during our daytime hours will also be dominant when we sleep. If we keep our mind focussed on what is good or positive, pure and tranquil nature, the rest of our lives will become serene and filled with joy.

"In peace I will lay down and go to sleep in your presence alone. O LORD, let me rest in peace." (Psalm 4:18)

In this passage, we can see that the LORD God of heaven will make us rest in peace while we go to sleep. We shouldn't be afraid to go to bed due to the possibility of experiencing nightmares, because He will make our sleep be tranquil.

"If you lay down you won't be scared and when you lay down you will sleep sweet." Proverbs 3:24

Isn't that a wonderful promise? "When you go to bed to sleep, it will be sweet." Keep in mind that if you are focused on God and all good things, You can have"Sweet" sleep, not an uneasy or gruelling sleep.

What is the Bible Says about Nightmares, Dreams, and Insomnia

"Do not take the road of the wicked and don't walk the path of evil. Do not take it on; leave it behind and continue through. Because they can't sleep unless they've committed a sin or if they have been robbed of sleep unless they've caused someone to fall." (Proverbs 4:4-16)

There are two main phrases found in these verses. The firstone is "Cannot rest," while the other is "robbed from sleep." The two words are clear indications that someone who pursues a negative path through their life that triggers negative Neurological thinking patterns will experience insomnia. In many psychological disorders , insomnia is a frequent occurrence in those who are. Sleeping disorders can cause psychological symptoms such as fatigue, irritability and inability to concentrate, be focused, anxiety, depression, hallucinations, psychosis and a decrease in the capacity to process thought in a rational manner, and loss of joy and decrease the efficiency of everyday tasks.

If we examine what Neurological impacts of insomnia using an FMRI scan we observe an reduction in activity within the Neocortex. When there is less activation within the Neocortex our cognitive abilities, decision making, and higher level of reasoning is severely diminished. This means that when our inferior cerebral cortex (Limbic System) which includes our Amygdala is activated too much, it results in a diminished ability to manage our emotions. This can lead to excessively active impulses, a rise in craving, and a rise in anxiety, fear depression, stress and depression.

The influence of angels on our neurological System when we are awake and when we are in a dreaming state

Numerous times, angels has been able to meet God's people with visions, dreams or even appearing in person. They've all appeared to give messages about the future events as well as encouragement and messages of salvation and salvation. They've come to help in fighting battles and to defeat the enemy that is coming against God's people.

"Are these not ministering spirit-filled beings who are sent out to serve the cause of those who will receive salvation." (Hebrews 1:4)

In this passage, we can clearly observe that the angels are sent for us to assist and to minister to us. They are able to be with us, interact with us, and convey messages that God desires us to receive and comprehend. Let's take a look at some examples of angelic interventions in the Bible:

Peter Released through Jesus Christ by Angel from the LORD

In the time of unleavened bread, The king Herod defeated James who was the son of

John the apostle, using the sword. He noticed that this was arousing the Jewish people, and then went on to arrest Peter as well. He then placed him in a jail with four guards to protect him. But the soldiers were nothing against the LORD who instructed His angel to save Peter.

"And behold an angel of the LORD was standing near his side, as well as a bright light displayed in the cell. He hit Peter with his side of his body and awakened him, telling him to "Get up fast" The chains were removed from his hands. as they passed by the first and the second guard and came to the iron gate that was leading into the city. It opened for them on its own volition and they walked out and walked along one street. Then the angel disappeared." (Acts 12:7 12, 10)

Apostles Freid through An Angel by the Lord

"But the high priest rose , along with all those who were together with him, and became enthralled with jealousy. They took the apostles into custody and placed them in a public prison. In the evening, when an angel from the LORD came through the prison gates and led them out. He declared, "Go and stand in the temple and teach people the whole language of this world." When they received this message, they went into the temple at the break of dawn and began to instruct." (Acts 5:17-21)

Thus, the angel of God appeared to them clearly and opened the prison doors and gave them instructions for them to go to the temple to continue to preach the Scriptures of God and an enlightening light which entered this world to conquer the enemy , so that we could be at peace.

"The Angel Gabriel Appeared to Mary

There was a virgin who's title was Mary. She was engaged to get with a guy called Joseph. The angel appeared in Mary and handed her an angelic message to the LORD:

"Greetings O you who is favored The LORD has been with you! Don't be scared Mary because you have been blessed by God. In the future, you will have a baby in your womb, and give birth to a son. you'll name him Jesus. He will be big and will be referred to as"the son of God the most high. Also, the LORD God will give him the seat that his grandfather David and he will rule over Jacob's house Jacob for eternity, and in his reign there will never be an ever ending." Then Mary asked her angels "How do I know this because I am pregnant?" And the angel replied, "The Holy Spirit will be overshadowing you, and the baby to be born will be referred to as holy, The God's Son. God. Behold, your cousin Elizabeth aged 87 also had a child and it will be the 6th month of her, and she was known as barren. Because nothing is impossible when it comes to God." and Mary declared, "Behold, I am the one who serves the LORD Let it happen to me in accordance with your instructions." And the angel left the woman." (Luke 1:16-38)

Wow! What is a message that could be delivered by an angel! So, it was that Mary was born and soon to be husband Joseph was able to find out. Joseph was a decent and honest man, and was did not want to be shamed by Mary. He was planning to divorce Mary without a fuss.

"But when he was contemplating these things, he saw one of the angels from God the LORD came to him through the form of a (dream) and said to him "Joseph Joseph, son of David don't be afraid to accept Mary to be your bride, because the conception that is in her is the work of God's Holy Spirit. She will have an infant and you'll be able to call him Jesus and Jesus will redeem those who love him from iniquities." As Joseph awakeed from his sleep did what an angel from the LORD instructed that he take his bride." (Mathew 1:20-21 1:14)

An angel from God the LORD was seen in a vision in a dream, as Joseph was lying in bed asleep. Therefore, it is evident that angels may appear to us in dreams, bringing instructions to us from God. God and save us, engage in discussions with us, address questions and even touch our bodies to awake us from our deep sleep, open doors unblock gates, remove chains that are in our hands and encourage us. They appear in person as well as in dreams. Now , we know the Biblical truth about angels' ability to influence our thoughts actions, freedom thoughts, thoughts and dreams.

Therefore, the problem now is: What is the status of the 1/3 of angels who were in heaven at the time that Lucifer was rebelling against God? Are they still able influence us in the same way as other angels who didn't resist God were and are now able to?

The answer is yes. We have to accept it as a fact and be prepared to defend ourselves in the visions, dreams, ideas, and guidance that fallen angels provide us. Let's take a examine the way God places his angels in the ranks.

Angelic Order According to Scripture

The Bible clearly demonstrates that angels are a variety of angels who perform different tasks. There are particular missions they perform based on their position in heaven. As the ranks exist among the good angels, there are ranks among fallen angels also. However, for the moment, we will concentrate on the order of angels who are good in the Bible.

Classification among The Angelic Order:

1.) Cherubim in the Bible: The Cherubim were used in which something had to be secured, for example the entrance to Eden's Garden. Eden."So he drove away the man, and set up to the east end of the garden of Eden Cherubim and an flaming sword that was turned in every direction in order to protect the way from the tree of eternal life." In the times of Moses it was written"The Cherubim shall spread out their wings, and overshadow the mercy seat with their wingsand faces facing one another. towards the mercy seat should be the face of Cherubim appear." (Exodus 25:20) The mercy seat was set over the ark , with Cherubim on the mercy seat as a symbol for Cherubim's protection of the Ark of God his holy throne.

Moses even provided instruction regarding which image Cherubim was to be weaved into the ten curtain panels in the tabernacle, which was used to safeguard from the Ark of God (see Exodus 26:1-3). The usage in the Cherubim to symbolize for the protection of His Ark and His garden demonstrates that God has set these angels up as Guardians. They are often referred to in the modern world as Guardian Angels.

2.) 2.) The Seraphim 2.) The Seraphim (Isaiah 6:2) it is written"Above him was the Seraphim. They each had six wings. With two wings, he covered his face. With two, he covered his feet and with two, he flew. One of them called out to the other and stated: "Holy, holy, holy is the LORD of hosts! The whole world is filled with the glory of his name!" The Seraphim are distinct from the Cherubim in that they sat above the Kingship of God and performed hymns of praise and worship towards the LORD. The Cherubim are the ones who guard the throne. In this case, we can observe how the Seraphim stood above God worshipping Him and not defending Him. They are the angels who lead heaven's worship to our God of the universe. Let's take a look at the words of Lucifer"Thou is the anointed guardian cherub who covers thee; and I have made thee as I have set: thou wast on God's holy mountain. God" (Ezekiel 28:14).

Therefore, we can now see how Lucifer was among the guardians of the Cherubim who were guardians of the reign of God. However, God created Lucifer distinct from other Cherubim of the Guardians. He gave Lucifer "Tabrets" and"Pipes." They are instruments for music that were utilized in the making of music. Therefore, not only was he guardian, he was an instructor in worship just similar to the Seraphim. God made him an amazing angel with many capabilities that were not available to counterparts in angels. He was made to be half Cherubim and half Seraphim. The one who worships and the guardian! Let's take a examine the words Lucifer stated in his heart,"For it is written in your heart that I will ascend to heaven, I will raise my throne over all the stars that are in God I will be in the mount of congregations, in the north's ridges I will rise above the clouds' heights and I will become as high as the Supreme".

In the Bible, it says that He would"ascend in the heavens above stars created by God" He is referring to the angels who are above God as well as Seraphim. They wanted to rise greater in comparison to God as well as his followers to ensure that God would be in his place and the worshipers of God, the Seraphim were also worshippers of Lucifer.

3.) The Living Creatures 3. The Living Creatures (Revelations 6:1) it is written"I I heard one of the living creatures call out "come" using a sound as thunder." In (see Revelations 6:1-8) it is clear it is clear that these"living living creatures" are angels who announce and direct the judgments of God in the final days.

4.) The Archangels The Archangels: In the Book of (Enoch 20:1-7) it lists six different angels who possessed the title and power as an Archangel. These include Uriel, Raphael, Raguel, Gabriel, Michael, Lucifer and Zariel. The meanings behind their names are listed below: Uriel (God is my light), Raphael (God heals), Raguel (Friend of God), Gabriel (God is my strength), Michael (Who is the same as God?), Lucifer (Morning star or Light-bringer) And Zariel (Lion in the name of God). It is mentioned in (Tobit 12:15) Raphael is mentioned"I am Raphael One of seven angels that serve to God in the Glory of God. Lord", who was shaken to the core by the sound of their voices, they collapsed in terror. However, Raphael spoke to his companions "Do don't be scared; be at peace! God bless you! God today and for eternity."

In the Holy Scriptures Gabriel and Michael are referenced in (Daniel 8:16 9:21) and (Revelation 12:7). The Bible mentions the "seven angels" multiple times throughout"Revelation." In (Revelation 8:2) it is written,"And I saw the seven angels which stood before God; and to them were given seven trumpets" and in (Revelation 15:1) it is written,"And I saw another sign in heaven, great and marvelous, seven angels having the seven last plagues, which would bring God's wrath to completion". The seven angels who mention in (Revelation) are the seven angels mentioned in the Bible books (Enoch as well as Tobit.) The archangels have authority and have been given specific tasks to guard and help God's holy people as well as to combat the enemies for God's people.

The Bible says in (Daniel 10:21) it's written that,"But I will show you that which is recorded in the word of truth There is no one who can be my ally in these things but Michael the prince of your heart." In this passage we can see how Michael has been declared to be a"Prince." In addition In (Daniel 10:13) there an angel who appeared to give a message for Daniel as well. The angel told him to Daniel that"But"the prince from the Kingdom of Persia stood up to me for twenty-two days; But, lo, Michael, one of the princes of the highest rank, appeared to my aid; and I stayed there with the King from Persia". From this single verse we can determine the fact that Michael is the Archangel has been identified as a"Chief Prince" and he engaged in battle with the"Prince of Persia." The angel who was in the same room with Daniel was separated from the"Kings of Persia" until Michael was able to free that angel so they could follow the desires of God.

In the kingdom of the enemy, there are princes and kings. The fallen angels of the rebels fight God's Archangels in an attempt to stop the Archangels from carrying out their purpose. Lucifers angels fight with God's archangels to stop us from receiving messages God sends to His people.

5.) The Watchers 5.) The Watchers (Daniel 4:13) it's written,"I was able to see in the visions of my head on my bed, and behold, a watcher as well as an holy person came down from the heavens" and the scripture (Daniel 4:17) it is written,"This situation is determined due to the order of the watchers and the the words from the Holy Ones to the purpose that the living might be aware that the Most High is the ruler of the realm of the world, and grants it to whomever he pleases and gives over the lowest of human beings." By this verse we learn that watchers are"Holy ones." The watchers are angels who have the ability to issue an order, and with their word, it's done Do you recognize that? Our Supreme court, our legislations and congress, judges and legislators are the ones who make the decisions and sentences. The Watchers are heaven's form of legislation, judges and congress.

6.) 6.) The Sons of God The Sons of God is recorded in(Job 1:6) "Now there was a time when they Sons of God arrived to stand to their LORD and Satan was also present." It was also mentioned in (Job 2:1). was recorded on (Job 2:1) "again there was a day that the Sons of God arrived to present themselves to the LORD and Satan joined them to be presented to God the LORD." The Bible it is apparent that"Sons of God" is the general name for all angels. The majority of angels is called"Sons of God." Each kingdom has a number of subjects. The angels are most likely God's divinely-appointed subject population.

Angelic Hierarchy:

* Cherubim * Cherubim (Guardians of the Lord)

* Seraphim * Seraphim (Worshipers worshippers of God)

* The living Creatures (Announce God's judgments)

*The Archangels (God's battle Angels)

*The Watchers (God's government)

"Sons" of God * Sons of God (General Anglican Population)

Angelic Abilities

Even though those fallen angels have been thrown out of heaven, it does not mean that they have lost their angelic power. Don't underestimate your adversaries. Let's take a examine the capabilities of angels, both good or evil angels.

Outline of the Good Angelic Abilities of the Lord's Angelic Host

* Can open doors.

* Can appear in dreams.

* Can appear in plain sight.

* Could warn of trouble.

* Will fight for us.

* Can encourage us.

* Physically assist us.

* Can be freed from us.

* Do not have names.

"Follow God.

* It is possible to call upon to assist in Jesus the name of Jesus.

* The ability to commission.

* Accept Jesus as Savior and Lord

• Praise and Worship God

* Can minister.

* Are true.

* Increase the strength.

* We are strengthened by Jesus' name. Jesus.

* Speak encouraging words.

"* Are You Good (positive).

The Enemy's Fallen Angel Host

* May move things and even open doors.

* May appear in dreams.

* Can appear in plain sight.

* It could be the cause of problems.

* Can battle against good angels.

* Can battle against us.

* It can be frightening for us.

* Could physically hurt us.

* Can torment us.

* Do not have names.

"Follow the enemies.

* It is possible to be thrown out and tossed removed in Jesus in Jesus' name.

* Can be removed or commanded to leave, and then removed.

* Deny Jesus.

* Honor the enemy.

* Can deceive.

* Are liars.

* The mockery and ridicule.

* Scream and are afraid by Jesus' name. Jesus.

* Speak destructive words.

* Are evil (negative).

How do be sure that the vision, dream or thought isn't from or an Angel or the Lord? It is simple to determine. The message in a demon-related dream, vision or thought is that of a destructive, negative nature, urging you to perform something or experience something that goes against the principles of Christ. In the beginning and throughout the process of writing this book, I was plagued by nightmares where spirits of the devil would visit me, torture me, afflict me and make me fearful. However as the nightmares kept appearing, I was able to see what was going on in the dream and make a the conscious choice during my sleep to confront the demons by telling them, "In Jesus name I have you removed or require to go away in Jesus the name of Jesus." If I were to perform this in my dreams, I'd witness that all the power of the gods would be removed from my sight then peace would come back and I would be awake.

I've been thinking for an extremely long duration "Why do these demons show up so often in my dreams, and annoy me day after the night?" When I came to the conclusion of why they appeared, I had a second dream. In the dream , I was at a desk and was handed this lengthy endless scroll. I was told by an unidentified voice to write down on this scroll everything I knew and knew about demons. After I had written everything down and was finished the work, it was removed from my desk by an force so powerful that it shook me awake in my dream. Then, the scroll was sent out to the world." The moment I awoke awake from my dream, I was aware of what I was supposed to do. I was to write this book and expose the enemies. This is me writing everything I have learned about Neurological combat so that it will be released out to the world and aid you in understanding the enemy, so you can take back the control of your Neurological system and return it to the state God wanted it to be in.

I'm going to write about an experience that I had during my stay in an institution. I was prescribed a drug that led to the inability to walk. It was a horrible result. I was admitted to an inpatient hospital for intensive physical therapy. I was working on the book for a total of 25 days. I had accomplished so much at this point. I began to have nightmares every night while I worked on it, and each nightmare was about demonic beings invading my life and causing me to suffer. There was one particular vision that was distinct among all the others and I'm going to reveal it to you. In the dream, I was lying on my bed in a hospital as I saw women in their bed. There was a loud thud of the door, a growl, and a scratch on the doors. The demon was trying to gain entry to the door, and could only get it open to a small crack. The entity was unable to get inside because I had put a prayer over the door to keep evil spirits out.

I was praying in the dream, and then threw it away in Jesus in Jesus' name. my thoughts were during the dreams "Well I can't let it be in my dream so I'm going to bed. I'm secure today." I realized that I was in reality just after the dream. The moment I awoke, there was a woman in the middle of my room just in front of my bed. She was facing my bed. As soon as that I started asking her whether she's fine and she fell to her back and began to convulse upon the ground. In the dream, the enemy couldn't penetrate me the way the way he had hoped to. He fought someone who was less strong on the faith side. The woman who fell was a negative character who was not a believer in God. Her weakness was the weaker person that would be attacked by the enemy. The enemy was attacking the woman immediately after the dream, it scared me. It made me realize that I was putting my life at risk by exposing the lives of people in my vicinity by writing this book.

Then I put down my pen and spoke with a Chaplain about what happened and my fears about continuing the writing process. He offered me some good tips and also prayed with me to direct my spirits to leave me and the people who were around me. The issue was that I was afraid. It was such an incredibly frightening event that I decided to stop writing the book. I let my anxiety of facing the adversaries keep me from writing the book God told for me to create. After I had stopped writing the book, the nightmares of the devil did not come. I didn't start writing this book once more after returning at home, living in a house filled with followers. I shouldn't have given up on writing the book. I shouldn't allowed the terror of the adversaries distract me from the task God has given me. That's why I will not cease writing this book regardless of what the enemy might throw at me.

I am more confident in my faith and believe in God to guide me and shield me from the evil one. Don't let your worries take over your life to the point where you cease doing the things you're doing for the Lord. He will safeguard you, guide you, and be with you through the whole process. Don't undervalue the potential that your dream can bring to you. Many scientists believe that dreams are merely the collective expression that our imagination creates from our daily and even our past experiences. As you're aware, there is a battle going on in your neurological system, which is trying to make it not function correctly, to cause psychological issues and to cause you to suffer from physical ailments that are triggered by stress.

The Bible clarifies:

"For God speaks in one manner, and in two ways, even though man does not see the message. A dream occurs an image of night in which deep sleep falls on the men as they lay in their bed, God opens the ears of men and terrorizes them with warnings that could turn man away from his actions and hide his pride from the man" (Job 33:14-19)

God communicates with us through dreams. Sometimes, it is an instruction from God or a message from God that angels deliver or sends, and other times it's the vision of an event which is scheduled to take place in the future. Dreams are the ones that God gives you and wants you to interpret also. Request God to clarify the meaning of your dreams and assist you understand the meaning before going to sleep at night , or immediately after having an experience. God will be able to answer your prayers with guidance and help toward the correct answer.

"Call me and I'll answer and reveal to you amazing and powerful things you do not know." (Jeramiah 33 3)

Chapter 5: The Instinctive Brain

The part that is instinctual of the Neurological system is located in the lower portion in your brain. It's known as the primitive brain. The brain is responsible for controlling instinct-driven emotional reactions, which all connect to survival in the first place. It is responsible for fear, hunger and sexual desires. If someone is under the influence of a demon negative thoughts can occur. this section within the Neurological system could result in unhealthy cravings for food and sexual desire. The demonic entity may create thoughts inside our minds that can be apprehensive concerning sex or food, as well. And if the one who is in the grip of it doesn't get these thoughts away then they will take over the person and cause an unhealthy addiction.

If someone is able to allow these thoughts to occur, it can lead to obesity, anorexia or bulimia. This may lead to ketoacidosis, malnutrition, diabetes and congestive heart failure high blood pressure , and eventually death. However an unhealthy sexual appetite could lead to diseases like AIDS, Gonorrhea, Herpes, Chlamydia, and multiple other sexually transmitted illnesses.

Let's take a look at what Bible describes about the natural person:

"These people are blaspheming everything they don't comprehend and are ruined by everything they, like animals with no rational thought know intuitively" (Jude 10, p.)

"These are snarls, malcontents and snobs who are following their sexual desires. They are loud mouthed boasters using their privilege to gain an advantages" (Jude 16)

They don't seem like genuine nice people Do they? Hearing "Loudmouth boasters" make me want to sprint as quickly that I am able in the other direction. The Bible specifically calls these types of individuals "unreasoning animals" thus the name (Reptilian Brain) that scientists have given to the lower brain. It is named after the word "unreasoning species."

"But they, like other uninformed creatures, animals of instinct, created to be snatched and destroyed in their blasphemy over things of which they have no knowledge they will also be destroyed by the destruction of their actions being wronged due to their infractions. They take pleasure in the fact that they take pleasure in the daylight. They're blemishes, blots and revel in their deceit while they eat and drink with you. They are awash in sexual immorality, and are insatiable to commit be sinning. They lure insecure souls. They are trained by desire." (2 Peter 2:12-14)

By allowing this "Instinctual thoughts" get in your head, you could cause you to self-destruction. That's exactly what the enemy wants your mind to think! After you have uncovered the strategy of the enemy for your subconscious mind, you are able to eliminate those kinds of thinking and substitute them for the words of God and words of PEACE, LOVE and Joy. Be firm with the Truth and you'll triumph over the enemy with a mighty victory. Be strong, my sisters and brothers because the tactics and strategies of the enemy are being exposed to you, so that you can defeat them! Be encouraged!

How to recognize Instinctive Thoughts

Instinctual thoughts are those that are involuntary filled with anger, anxious, and show an unhealthy craving for excessive indulgence in drugs, food or sexual activity. These are thoughts that suggest the ability to control things, people or things. They suggest to be fearful and to be a fighter or escape in certain circumstances where there is no threat to your life. Sometimes , these thoughts are naturally positive like:

* A bear is moving towards you and you should flee.

* You have to fall in the effort to love your partner in order in order to create.

* You must take a meal since you're hungry.

* You must work to the max at your job, so that you can feed your family and securely protect your family.

* This is considered as a risky area and you should never let your car open without locking it or leave the vehicle at all.

However, at times these thoughts may be negative for example:

It's delicious. It is imperative to eat the whole of it and even order more since you might never have it ever again.

All of these women are stunning. You should sleep with as many women as you want.

* Do not venture to the woods, as there are animals waiting around to harm me.

141

* Don't leave your home since there are murderers criminals, and rapists on the loose.

* Don't go to areas that are crowded because the majority of people will try to harm you.

* Your wife disrespected you. Let her know who's boss.

Beat your wife to ensure she is under your control.

Thinking that is of an instinctual nature , and that are controlled by a demon are extremely fearful or nervous, filled with anger and revenge, as well as obsessed when it comes to sexuality, food greed, control, and power They will be obsessed in retaining control and power over all aspects of your life. in extreme situations the thoughts may turn suicidal, homicidal or both. If thoughts of this kind occur in your mind, you should immediately acknowledge these thoughts, rebuke them in Jesus in Jesus' name, and remind yourself of the good and positive aspects of the circumstances you're in.

The enemy would like you to react instinctively and not think rationally. He would like to concentrate your thoughts in your lower part of your brain and not in the upper part of your brain which uses reasoning abilities to get through any circumstance. Consider asking yourself "How can I demonstrate my trust in the word of God and His love to those in this circumstance?"

"In every circumstance, you must take that shield with faith that will ward off any flaming darts of the devil." (Ephesians 6:16)

The "Darts" are negative thoughts that come to you. And the"Shield of faith" is the belief about the GOD-child! He is your protector regardless of the situation. It is your faith in His faithfulness and the confidence that you don't have anything to worry about, and not to worry about and that you've been given the full authority over your enemies and you will not be harmed by anyone.

Intuition or the Holy Spirit

Intuition is the term used to describe knowledge and comprehension that is beyond what you've learned during your entire life. It can tell the difference between both positive and detrimental. It will help you understand the emotions of others whether they're either happy or sad. It can tell that something is coming up and can tell when people are lying.

Sometimes, it will let you know that somebody is looking at you, or even when you are about to speak to you.

This guide tells youto "Don't visit the location you're considering going because something dangerous is set to occur". It provides you with a sense that everything happens to be for a reason or an understanding that the person who is in front of you is your true love. If your partner cheats on you with a different person, it is likely that you know this is taking place because your instincts have already warned you that something isn't quite right regarding what your partner does or declares. It's what people consider to be "red signals" that could be described as intuitional understanding. This guide also provides what we'd like to refer to as"an "epitome" also known as "creative thoughts" that appear out of thin air. This guide is what triggers many , if not all, discoveries in science and inventions of different kinds. Let's take a examine what the Bible says regarding this so-called intuitiveness...

Jesus declared:

"These things I've spoken to you in my time still in your midst. However, the helper, The

Holy Spirit who the Father will send to me in my name, will instruct you in all matters as well as bring to Remembrance everything I've told thee." (John 14:25,26)

According to this verse it's stated in the Bible that Holy Spirit guides us. He also helps us remember what we've learned. He is our friend who is sent by our Father in heaven.

"And when he returns and convicts the entire world of sin, righteousnessand judgment. When the Spirit of Truth appears to guide you, he will lead you to the truth in all things because he does not declare his authority on his own however, whatever he hears, the Lord will say, and he will tell you about the things to be revealed. Jesus will be glorified because he will take the things that belong to me and proclaim the truth to your ears. (John 16:8, 13-15)

In this passage, the Holy Spirit is stated to "convict all people of the sin of righteousness and the judgment" Does this not seem like an intuition or sub-conscious? It gives you a sense of the difference between what is good (righteousness) as well as bad (sin) and providing you with the ability to discern whether something someone is real or is a lie."He will lead you to the truth in all things."

Jesus declared He said the Holy Spirit would "Declare to you what is to be." That means He will inform you of what's going to happen in the near future. Like intuition when you feel that something is coming up or something tells you to call home, because something isn't just right. You might be asking yourself, "I have never felt extremely intuitive. Does this mean that the Holy spirit isn't in my being?" The answer to that is yes. However, only if you've not taken on Christ as Savior and Lord.

The text reads:

"'Let everyone in the house of Israel be aware for certain that God has created him as LORD and Christ Jesus, the Jesus who you crucified. Then when they heard this, they were shattered to the core and asked Peter and the other apostles, "Brothers, what do you do?' Peter told them to repent and be baptized by every person in honor of Jesus Christ for the forgiveness of your sins and you will be granted the blessing from the Holy Spirit. The promise is made for you as well as your children, and to all who are away, anyone who God of our God invites to his own.'" (Acts 2:36-39)

This is the method to be redeemed and the receiving by Holy Spirit: Holy spirit:

* Turn away from sin to accept Christ as your Lord and Savior. (Say this in your soul and say it aloud)

* Be baptized in Christ's name. Jesus Christ.

* Get the gift of the Holy Spirit.

"The Spirit helps us in our weaknesses. We don't know what to pray about like we should to, but the Spirit himself prays for us, groaning in a way that is that are too profound to express in to be expressed in words." (Romans 8:26)

And even if we are unsure of the best option for us based on our own experience, God's Holy Spirit intercedes for us to get everything we need.

"Now we have not received"The Spirit from the outside, but rather the Spirit that comes from God so that we can be able to comprehend the gifts freely given to us through God." (1Corinthians 2:22)

God's Spirit of God communicates the deepest profundity of the knowledge God is able to provide. However, it is also true that the Holy Spirit can be selective in the knowledge he chooses to give the believers.

"To everyone is that manifestation by the Spirit to promote to promote the good of all mankind. Because to one person is by the Spirit the expression of Wisdom and to another, the imparting of knowledge in accordance with the same Spirit and to another faith, by this same spirit and to another performing of miracles, to another prophesy, the ability to differentiate between spirits, and another, the interpretation of tongues. All of these are given from the spirit of the Lord who distributes to each in a particular way according to what he wishes." (Corinthians 12:7-11)

Let's take a look at the many similarities in Intuition and the Holy Spirit and Intuition:

Holy Spirit

* Teach all subjects.

* Helps you to know the truth.

* Declares future events.

* Convicts all the world of righteousness and sin.

* Makes an honest judgment of everything.

* Provides insight into the truth and the lies.

* Helps us when we aren't sure what to do.

* Provides insight into specific abilities that aren't learned.

* Shares knowledge that was never acquired.

* Provides an idea of inspiration.

* Helps us with everything.

Intuition

* Reveals hidden knowledge.

* Uncovers the truth.

* Unveils the future.

* Explains to you the distinction in right and wrong.

• Describes the way to judge things.

* Helps distinguish between lies and truth.

This article explains what to do when we don't be sure of the best course.

* Provides an idea of inspiration.

* Helps to understand the abilities you have never had prior to

* Gives knowledge as gifts.

* Aids us in everything.

We have now looked at the many similarities between both the Holy Spirit and the intuition It is safe to claim that intuition is the work of the Holy Spirit and that intuition is merely man's method of explaining what he can not comprehend. The direction we receive is God communicating to us via the Holy Spirit, and we need to believe in the Holy Spirit of God to guide us in the right direction.

Holy Spirit or the Spirit of the Antichrist

We've learned that the Holy Spirit can be described as God's Spirit of God that leads us into every truth. Lucifer is also a spiritual being and is known as"the Spirit of the Anti-Christ. The spirit guides us through the path of deceit and error.

"'Beloved Beloved, don't believe any spirit, but test the spirits to see if they come from God In this way, you can identify that you are in the Spirit of God and every spirit that claims that Jesus Christ is the Christ who has come in flesh is from God and any spirit that refuses to acknowledge Jesus is not of God. The spirit that is leading the Antichrist."' Through this, we can discern what is the Spirit Of Truth and the spirit of error." (1 John 4:1-3 4:6)

As the Holy Spirit communicates with us and directs us as well, so do the spirits of antichrist. There is a thing that is common that binds both the Holy Spirit as well as that of antichrist, and it can be found in the Neurological system. Both help us to think through our thoughts. The Holy Spirit is our guide in all positive things, and the antichrist guides us in everything negative. The Holy Spirit is our guide but that spirit called the antichrist is adamant about bringing us down with savage accusations. You may be wondering, "How can I tell what spirit is communicating with me?" I have placed an outline below to aid you to understand the distinction between these two.

Holy Spirit

"You are the loved God's child. God.

Don't forget to exercise your power in Christ.

You are a victor.

"You are loved by everyone..

* You can.

* You deserve being loved.

* You can count on God in any circumstance.

* Relax, everything will be okay.

"You are mighty soldier for Christ.

* Help those around you who are in pain.

* Forgive your enemy.

* You are perfect.

* You are gorgeous.

* You are smart.

You are significant to God.

* Christ is our Lord and Savior.

Spirit of the Antichrist

* God is not the one who truly loves you.

What authority? You're weak!

* You're a complete failure.

* Everyone is against your name and speaks about you in secret.

* You cannot

Do you really think that anyone can truly love you?

* How do you believe in to a God who allows you to be a victim?

* Do not be afraid.

* You're not powerful.

* Don't think about your friend. He was not with you when you needed him.

* Retribute your adversaries.

* You are not perfect.

"Your fat, ugly and ugly

* You're a fool.

* You're not smart.

* God doesn't even care about you.

* Christ is not anything.

Do you see the difference between the way that the Holy Spirit influences your thinking as well as how the mind of antichrist is guiding your thoughts? Any thought that enters your mind that has an insulting nature comes of the enemy. The thoughts of the enemy are always trying create a feeling of weak and insignificant. It's time to fight negative thoughts and take back you Neurological system. God will be with you throughout the process. It may not be straightforward at first, but after a while, you will be a optimistic, joyful, and caring God's child. God. Don't allow the enemy to prevail! You are the one who controls these thoughts. Don't let them control your nervous system, which could result in a psychological disorder. It is possible to do this. I am confident in you!

What is the impact of the enemy's goal on Your Relationships and Life

If the enemy gains an uncontrollable grip on your life, it can make you feel invincible over all the circumstances, making your mind turn to be a victim mindset. The thoughts you'll start to experience are those of hopelessness and helplessness , for example:

* I'm not able to get to get out.

* I'm a complete failure.

* I am weak.

* I am incompetent.

* Nobody will ever be able to love me.

* I am not wanted.

* I have no value or worth or.

* I am large and ugly.

* I'm not attractive or attractive enough.

"My situation seems hopeless.

* I'm going to be lonely for the rest of my life.

* Nothing is ever perfect for me.

* There's no reason to even attempt to make myself better. I'm a loser.

What is the reason I should use the techniques I'm learning from this book. There's no way to fix me.

The enemy would like you to be an uninformed victim and never discover what you really are in Christ. The enemy would like you to believe that there is nothing to assist you in the difficult situations you encounter. But the truth is that you're more than capable of being all you want to be! You're someone who's in the direction of victory! It is only a matter of declaring that victory . Only then do you stop thinking of yourself as a victim. You'll walk with more confidence and you will be more self-sufficient, and you will be successful.

"Who will keep us from the lovingkindness of Christ? Do we need to endure tribulation, or suffering or persecution, hunger, or vulnerability or even swords? In all of these, we are greater than conquerors thanks to Jesus who loved us." (Romans 8:35 and 8:37)

There is more to you than just a conqueror! You are a winner! Whatever has been your experience in the past, it doesn't have for you to be a part of your. LOVE defines you; VICTORY defines you! When you stay within the "Victim" mindset, you are in a position to not be able to sustain healthy relationships as you anticipate the worst from all. These examples show people who have unhealthy mental thoughts that stem from a victim-based mindset:

* My wife is the only one who stays with me, because she is a bit petty about me and not because she loves me.

* I am the only one who leaves at the end, so why to try.

* I've been hurt in such a way that it has made me unimportant.

* I'm not satisfied with my abusive relationship, but I don't deserve any more.

It's my fault that he beats me because I'm not enough.

* Who could ever truly be able to love me? I am not anything.

When thoughts such as these pop up into your thoughts, remove them in Jesus Name and remind yourself how worthy and victorious you are. Remind you "I have earned the love of God and all good things!"

Things To Note:

* Your thoughts can influence your relationships.

Your thoughts can ruin the relationships you have with others if are in a victim-blaming mindset.

"You're a victor! A lot more than just a CONQUEROR in Christ Jesus!

* You are worthy of everything good!

* You don't have to allow debilitating thoughts to influence your feelings. You are in control of them!

What is the purpose of the enemy may affect your relationship with God

Lucifer isn't keen for you to know the extent to which your loved ones are respected by God. He would like you to feel lonely and unloved from the rest of humanity. He would like you to feel like you've been left out and disregarded by God. He will create thoughts in your head which will help you achieve this goal. These are some examples of thoughts sown by the enemy concerning the relationship you have with God:

* God isn't concerned with you.

* God allows you to suffer because He doesn't take care of you.

* He has turned you down.

*If God was a lover of you, then why did He allow those terrible things occur to you?

* God is not to be believed.

* God doesn't wish for you to think about yourself. He would like to rule you and take away your freedom.

* God isn't in fact.

The thoughts of all kinds concerning God create anxiety and fear. To be closer to God it is necessary to get rid of any thoughts that are of this kind. The enemy is trying to divert you from the God who is more loving than anything else. Although these thoughts can create the impression that there is an inequity between you and your relationship with God however, this isn't an actual fact. There is nothing that will hinder God from his love for you, not even Lucifers unsuccessful attempt to show His love as distinct from you.

"For I am certain that neither life nor death nor angels, neither rulers, nor anything in the present, nor things that are in the future, neither power and heights, nor depths or heights or anything else in the creation can separate us from the unconditional love that is the love of God with Christ Jesus Christ our Lord." (Romans 8:38 39)

The enemy can be able to fill you with thoughts of guilt and shame as a result of the many actions you've taken in your past that were negative in nature. They will tell you that:

* I am too bad for God to love me. God.

* How can God ever love someone as horrible as me.

* I'll never be sufficient to Him.

* I will never be forgiven for my actions.

" I'm a loved God's child. God? You must be lying to me.

"Everyone who trusts in Him will never be shamed" (Romans 10:11)

God would like to have an intimate relationship with God and you. He desires you to let your heart and your mind open to God. Don't fall for the lies of your enemies. God truly loves you and, even though we might not know His ways, they're made with ultimate good in the mind. It is possible that things at times seem unfair, but remember that God has plans to change everything to benefit you.

Chapter 6: The Demonic Possession

Through throughout the Bible there are many stories of possession by the devil. In this chapter, we're going to explore the psychological aspects of these possessions to know how the devil was able to influence the neurological system and central nerve system in the victim's. We know that they regard that the body of a human being as own home. They feel most comfortable and get the most pleasure. Let's look into what they are doing at Their "Home."

The enemy is attempting to attack you and your Neurological system with a single goal to gain the control of you. block your mind from understanding and truth of Christ Keep your from having a relationship with your Creator and then destroy your soul. The way the enemy achieves this is through the inception of thoughts into your mind which are destructive in nature. The enemy begins with demeaning thoughts , causing you feeling insecure and anxious, afraid or even rejected. If you allow these thoughts to linger, these thoughts will eventually become obsessive and develop into psychological disorders that could create severe emotional stress.

The psychological issues can affect you and can cause your capacity to fight back to decline considerably. Attacks against an Christians mind could result in oppression, but attacks on someone who is not a believer could result in total control where the person who is not a believer is controlled by the demon or entities. Let's look at the ways the enemy may manipulate victims they control:

Legion

"They went to the opposite shore of the sea in the country that was part of Gerasene's. And after Jesus had left the boat, immediately were in his tombs of a man who had an unclean heart. He was in the tombs. There was no way to bind him any longer and not even a chain because he had been chained with shackles and chains However, he tore the chains to pieces and tore the shackles in pieces. There was no one with the power to control him. All day and night, among the tombs and mountains, he was crying out and slicing himself in stones. When he observed Jesus from a distance then he ran to him and fell over before Jesus. and yelling out in an ebullient voice, he cried out: "What is it with me? Jesus Christ, the Christ, Son of our Most Exalted God?

I beg you by God don't torture me. Then he was telling him "Go out of the man, you filthy spirit!' Jesus asked him "What's your name?" He answered "My name is Legion as there are many of us. And he was determined to not take him out of the country. Then a large herd pigs was grazing on the hillside. they begged him saying"Send us to pigs, and let us go into them. Then, he granted them permission. And the spirits that were unclean came out into the pigs and the herd, which was approximately two thousand, rushed down the slope into the ocean and drowned in the sea.

The herdsman fled and explained it to the city in the countryside. Then the people came to investigate what that took place. And they went to Jesus and witnessed the man who was possessed by demons that was the one who had the legion sitting there covered in cloths and in his good mind, and were terrified." (Mark 5:1-15)

They may be possessed by humans and interfere with the neurological system, which causes the individual to exhibit suicidal behaviors or exhibit signs of psychosis and uncontrollable behavior. There may have more than one demon entity that seeks to take over the human. In this case , there was an entire legion of demonic entities within this person. A legion comprises 3000 entities. It was 3000 demonic entities which could possess only 1 Neurological system. The magnitude of this reality is astonishing. Possessions can trigger an absolute loss of self-control, or result in the person becoming extremely impaired. The actions of the non-believer who is possessed can be unpredictable, and they may cause injuries to their bodies as well as others.

Psychologists and Psychiatrists are today able to identify this person with some form of Psychosis or Schizophrenia with a tendency to engage in self-harm. They may even label him suicidal. They could have treated the man with anti-psychotic drugs together with other medications like mood stabilizers and anti-depressants. These could have aided in the reduction of these behavior as this type of medication could have helped to alter the neurologic system of his in a manner that would help reduce these behavior patterns and help calm his mind with its effects of sedation. In very high doses, this kind of medication might cause him to enter the Catatonic state, where the person would have been in an euphoriac state. He could have displayed an assault of non-responsiveness. It would not have corrected the problem, but it would be a cover for the issue.

Jesus told us, "Come out of the man, you filthy spirit." They left the man. The condition of the man afterwards could be described like this,"sitting in a robe, covered and in good spirits." It is evident that Jesus was the one who had the power to expel the spirits of the man. Jesus gave you the same authority to accomplish the identical. It is writtenin the Bible,

"And the following signs are going to come with those who believe in me: in my name , they will expel demons, they will speak with new tongues and they will catch serpents with their hands and if they drink poison that is deadly but it does not hurt them. They will also lay their hands on sick people and recuperate." (Mark:17-18)

It is not recommended to treat someone with mental illnesses or psychological problems. The faith in Christ and a knowledge of how you can regain your Neurological system could and will help you heal. You are able to be healed from any mental condition you are experiencing. If you implement the comprehensive methods that I will show you in the next chapter of the book. You will experience improvement in your mental health and be able to recover you Neurological System and bring it to the form the Creator had in mind for to have it.

Demonic Advantages Due to Insufficient Faith and Belief

"Some Jews who went around trying to expel evil spirits, attempted invoking the name God Jesus over people who were possessed by demons. They would say, "In God's name Jesus who Paul proclaims to be, I ask that you come out. Seven children of Sceva, who was a Jewish chief priest was doing this. The evil spirit came to them and said by saying, "Jesus I know and Paul I am familiar with however, what is your name? The man with the evil spirit jumped up on the entire group. He beat them so hard that they fled the house, bleeding and naked." (Acts 19:13-16)

The only way that the enemy could be able to see the Jews is through alteration of Occipital lobes, which gives humans visual perception. This enemy had the ability comprehend and verbally communicate its knowledge of Jesus and Paul through manipulating the Temporal Lobes the victim to ensure it could communicate by using the body of the victim. The Temporal lobes allow humans to have the capacity to create speech and to recognize. The enemy also altered the Premotor Cortex, causing the human body to "Jump over the entire body" and give"Them the kind of beating they received that they escaped the house, naked and bleeding." Premotor cortex

Premotor cortex provides a person with the ability to communicate motion in all the joints that make up his body. It only happens after a signal has been sent from the motor cortex via the Limbic system and then through the Brain stem to the body using Neurotransmitters that are signals that inform your body how to move.

If someone displays an aggressive behavior that causes one person hurts another or another person, they could be sent for anger-management classes and charged with a crime, or even incarcerated, or identified as having Bipolar disorder or Conduct disorder IBD or Oppositional defiance disorder. The majority of diagnoses of these kinds of disorders will involve an order for the beginning of treatment using mood stabilizers, sedatives as well as anti-psychotic medication. It was evident that the Jews had no connection with Jesus Christ and because of their incredulity or lack of trust in giving the demonic creature a command to get to leave the body, the demonic creature profited from this and physically attacked them. Faith and belief in Jesus are required to demonstrate this power. In numerous instances, Jesus stressed that faith is essential and belief in order for healing and miracles to occur. For instance:

"He said to her "Daughter! Your faith has restored you. Be at tranquility and free yourself from all your pain'." (Mark 5:34)

"Then Jesus said to him, "Rise and leave to the grave; your faith has brought you to health'." (Luke 17:19)

It is crucial to cultivate an belief that is rooted in Jesus Christ because if you are a believer, you can be healed and assist in helping to cure others from illnesses and the manipulation of the enemy. The enemy would like you to turn into an and unbeliever, because it knows that if you had faith, you would not be capable of defending itself with its strategies and tactics against you. If a person believes and believes in God, the Neurological system alters its neural network to force that belief into practice, which makes it more difficult for the enemy to influence you by presenting negative thoughts. It is a powerful thing to believe! The next tale about a demonic possession from the Bible affirms that faith is the only requirement to drive demonic entities out of your life:

Epileptic Spirit

" When they were greeted by the crowd, one man came towards Jesus and kneeled before Jesus. "Lord please have mercy on My son,"" the man said. "He suffers from seizures, and is suffering horribly. He is often thrown into the flame or the water. I took him to your disciples but they were unable to treat him." "O ignorant or perverse people! Bring this boy and see Jesus." Jesus replied. "How do I have to stay with you? What length of time must I endure with you? Bring him here for my house." And then Jesus confronted the demon and it was able to leave the boy. He was healed at that point. Afterward , the disciples came to Jesus privately and asked "Why could we not drive away the evil spirit?" "Because You have such a lack of faith," Jesus replied. "For truthfully, I'm telling that if you have the faith of a mustard seed, you can tell this mountain: 'Move this mountain from here to there' then it'll move. It will not be a problem for the person who has faith in you." (Matthew 17:14-20)

Even if you have heard of Jesus and follow Jesus as the disciples were following Him and you also be a believer in Jesus' power. Jesus. If we examine the way that the demon caused this child's behavior, we discern how it was making him to fall into fire as well as in the water. The boy would then to get severely burned or even to die and when we look at the way it hurling in the waters, you discern that it was attempting to submerge the kid. Modern-day doctors will determine that the child is epileptic, and prescribe him medications known as anti-seizure drugs. Seizures result from electrical signals sent by the neurologic system. When neurons transmit an array of signals simultaneously, the body can begin to show involuntary movement and emotional reactions that are involuntary. non-voluntary behavior, and muscles that are not moving and, in the case of seizures might even become unconscious.

The demon entity controlling the boy was able to alter the neurotransmitters within the brain's neuronetwork to create this type of behavior. Its goal was to trigger seizures in the child so that he'd drown or fall to his death, either through hitting his head or drowning and burning him to death. The enemy seeks to take over and it was obvious that the boy was suffering from the condition that modern doctors refer to as epilepsy, but in this instance it was a demonic entity intent on causing devastation to the body of the child. In the faith of God the demon can be banished out of inside the body of the patient. Numerous doctors attempt to deny this since they claim that it's an illness of the brain, and not linked to the demon, but this is a false assumption. The devil is able to fool all of humanity and doctors and scientists aren't in any way immune to this.

Be aware that not all with symptoms of this disease is affected, but everyone must pray for relief from the disease.

"Be mindful, remain vigilant as your foe is the devil, who roams about like a roaring lion looking for whom he can devour. Refuse him, remain with a firm faith in the (FAITH), knowing that the same troubles endured by your brothers around this world." (1 Peter 5:8-9)

A Mute Spirit

"And He cast out a demon and it spoke silent. It was at the time that the demon was gone and the mute had spoken, that the demon spoke and the crowds marvelled." (Luke 11:14)

There is a disorder known as "Selective Mutism." This condition can cause someone suffering from social anxiety to be unable to speak in certain social settings. It is caused by extreme anxiety that is so intense that the individual cannot speak. In many cases, a person who has selective mutism is able to talk to their family and friends close to them without issue but, in some instances it is the case that they cannot speak in any way. The enemy creates anxiety about speaking into their minds, causing the person to feel embarrassed trying to talk. This individual isn't mute because of Neurological issues or other problems with the development of their brain, but is affected by anxiety.

"For God has not given us the spirit of fear instead, he has given us power and love as well as a sound brain." (2Timothy 1:7)

God doesn't desire us to worry about anything. But the enemy does. He would like us to be anxious and stress that it ruins our bodies and minds so that it can lead to destruction. The spirit responsible for the muteness was likely an anxiety-based spirit or a fearful spirit. It can be dealt with by strengthening our belief to Jesus Christ so we can eliminate all thoughts that the enemy has for us which are of a tense or stress-inducing nature. The enemy can't cause us to be stressed or anxious. We must make the conscious choice to take these thoughts seriously and incorporate them into our everyday life.

"Do not be worried about anything. Instead, in all situations, through praying and petitioning and with gratitude, make your requests to God. The peace of God that transcends any comprehension, will protect your thoughts and your hearts with Jesus Christ Jesus." (Philippians 4:16-7)

Blind and Deaf Spirit

"And when Jesus appeared to His disciples, He noticed an enormous crowd of people around them, with Scribes arguing with them. The moment they came across Him, the people were amazed and ran towards Him, welcoming Him. Then, They asked Him "What are you talking about in your conversation with you?" Then one of the crowd members replied and said"Teacher, I've have brought my son to you who is mute. spirit. If it gets him, it hurls him to the ground; he screams in his mouth. He grinds his teeth and turns stiff. Therefore, I pleaded with your followers, asking them to could remove it however, they were unable to. Then he reacted and said: 'O faithful generation! How long will I remain with you? What is my time with you? I'll bring him before me. They then brought them to Him.

The moment He saw Him, the spirit began to shake him and he fell to the ground, and began to writhe in a rage of mouth. He then asked his father: 'How long ago has this happened for him? He he replied,'since childhood. He has often tossing him in the flame and into the water, threatening to kill the man. If you're able to accomplish anything, be kind on us

and assist and help us.' Jesus said to him: 'If you believe, everything is feasible for anyone who believes. The dad of the boy wept and cried out"Lord I believe; please aid my faithlessness! When Jesus observed that the whole crowd began to gather He confronted the unclean spirit by telling it "Deaf and dumb spirit I'm telling you to get away from me and go into the spirit's realm!' the spirit let out a cry and shook him violently and escaped from him. He was dead as a corpse and many people said"He's dead. Then Jesus took the man by the hand, and lifted him up and he got up. After He was brought to the house His disciples questioned Him privately, 'Why can't we not get rid of it?' Then He told those present, "This sort of thing can be removed with only prayers or the practice of fasting.'" (Mark 9:14-29)

There are similarities to the tale of the Epileptic spirit we talked about earlier. The spirit has similar traits to the spirit before. It is determined to kill him and then drown him. But the epileptic mind was in a position to be cured through faith. This deaf and dumb soul is only eliminated through prayer and fasting, not by faith by itself. To demonstrate actions that correlate to epilepsy, it has the capability of manipulating the electrical signals of the brain. It's bombarding with numerous signals simultaneously to cause the child to plunge into the fire and the water. Jesus was very clear in his statement that"This kind of thing can be overcome only through prayers or the practice of fasting." The practice of praying is type of meditation. If it is practiced consistently for three weeks or more, every day for 15 minutes, there are changes to the neurologic systems of a person suffering from the emotional disorders.

Prayer can trigger over-activity within the Amygdala (area of the brain that regulates emotions and emotional behavior) to reduce and boost activation within the

Frontal Lobe (area of brain that regulates positive emotions and behavior). Prayer can also change the brain's wiring by triggering Neuroplasticity to reinforce positive thoughts and behavior. If a person prays regularly for three weeks or more, the neurological system will function on behalf of the person suffering to reverse any negative thinking and behaviour patterns. Fasting, on the other hand, offers many benefits to the body both psychologically and physiologically. It is a great way to heal or reverse numerous illnesses. Studies have proven that fasting reduces the frequency of convulsions and assists in calming the neuron overactive ones by reducing the amount of signals permitted to travel through.

Ketones that are released into the blood due to fasting can help to relieve the convulsions. Thus, prayer and fasting will truly heal the person who is suffering from this condition. But what happens to the one who prays and fasts for the sick person? In fact, if someone regularly prays and fasts, the body and the brain will change like if they are the victims. The most important thing to note is the fact that when we repeatedly pray, your brain's higher part becomes more active while your lower brain is less active. This causes those who pray to be capable of focusing, concentrating on the problem, think, and perform better within the Frontal lobes. If this happens, your beliefs and faith are strengthened because of the speed of Neuroplasticity which reinforces your thoughts and belief systems.

It is therefore likely that the faith you have grows stronger as you pray, causing your brain to shift to the point to ensure that any commands that you make to the enemy are executed with a stronger faith and faith that triggers them to perform. Fasting can speed neural plasticity due to of the brain making ketones in place of glucose (sugar). If someone releases ketones in their blood, the brain performs superiorly than it does when it relies on glucose (sugar) to fuel its cells. If you pray and fast for people to be healed from an illness or a bad spirit, you'll develop more faith and belief which will enable you to eliminate it. More so than when you don't prayer or fast.

As we can observe in these Biblical instances of demon control, the devil has control over the Neurological system and manipulates it in an approach that causes the possessed to act in unsettling ways. We should remain aware of strategies and tactics of the adversaries when it comes to our neurological health. Our adversaries will seek to force negative thoughts upon you, and they can cause such a tyranny that they weaken you until your brain can be completely possessed.

"Be mindful and alert. The devil's foe prowls about like a roaring beast in search of a person to take in." (1 Peter 5:8)

Conclusion

This is the first step to the psychological warfare, the art of defeating and disarming your adversaries mentally. Within these chapters, you've learned a myriad of secret, dark and powerful techniques that let you mentally influence and harm others. You've learned how to increase that you are able to win any battle using an established and proven psychological strategy.

This book is now over however, your exploration into the dark art of psychological warfare doesn't need to end. You are able to continue using these techniques each day. Additionally, you can conduct further studies and get better in the art of psychological combat.

Psychological warfare isn't an entirely new idea. It's been in use for a long period of. Humans have always known that psychology is more potent and efficient than physical force and, as such, psychological warfare has been a popular component of conflict. It became a topic of interest to the public following World War II. In the end, most people aren't aware of the psychological conflict.

This is the reason why psychological warfare so powerful. It is difficult for people to realize that you're using these devious tactics against them. It's practically unknown and often not understood. Many dismiss these ideas as a conspiracy theory and do not believe the power of psychological combat. Make use of your ignorance to benefit you and allow them to be dumb while you take over their minds.

What you use this book for is completely your choice. It is possible to use it for harm. It is possible to utilize it to satisfy your simple and basic curiosity about more obscure concepts of psychology that mainstream psychology does not want you to know about. It is also possible to make use of this book to find ways to defend yourself and prepare yourself for future psychological battles. This book can certainly help you attain any of these goals.

However, after you read this book, you'll never ever be the same. The strategies described within these chapters will be in your mind. It is possible to begin applying them to great effect and not even realize it. When you reach the point where you are done, you have accomplished your goal by armed yourself with profound and effective techniques of psychological warfare that will enable you to win any battle you face anytime.

Psychological warfare is not an amusing or conspiracy theorist speculation. It's actually employed by government agencies and documented throughout the history of. In the age of the Internet and the Information Age, this form of war is more feasible and efficient. It is really possible to ruin lives by using psychological warfare, and reach more people via the power of propaganda now than at any time before. Don't undervalue the power of psychological warfare, or ignore it as something that can't possibly cause harm. It can.

Never underestimate the speed with which you can be victimized. Keep your eyes and ears open and treat everything with some caution. Don't sit in a state of utter helplessness, in the hope that things will be better when you're under psychological assault. The damage your mind can sustain due to psychological attacks is not a joke and your life could be irreparably damaged in the event that you don't immediately take action.

Thank you for taking time to read this. This book is definitely an extremely beneficial book you've ever read. It's already been a huge influence on you, and it will alter your life for good. Make use of it with care and observe how rapidly resistance will vanish and the things you desire are available to you.

.

www.ingramcontent.com/pod-product-compliance
Lightning Source LLC
Chambersburg PA
CBHW060331030426
42336CB00011B/1289